The *R* Option

Building RELATIONSHIPS as a Better Way of Life

MICHAEL SCHLUTER AND DAVID JOHN LEE

RELATIONSHIPS FOUNDATION

British Library Cataloguing in Publication Data
A record for this book is available from the British Library.

ISBN 0-9543879-0-2

Published by:
The Relationships Foundation
Jubilee House
3 Hooper Street
Cambridge CB1 2NZ
England
Tel: +44 (0)1223 566333
Fax: +44 (0)1223 566359
Email: r.f@clara.net
www.relationshipsfoundation.org

To our children
and grandchildren

CONTENTS

ACKNOWLEDGEMENTS 6

PREFACE 7

ABOUT THE AUTHORS 10

1. RELATIONSHIPS 17

2. TIME 23

3. COMMUNICATIONS 35

4. MANAGEMENT 47

5. MONEY 63

6. LUNCH 75

7. LEISURE 87

8. FRIENDS 97

9. SOUL MATES 107

10. SEX 119

11. LOSS 127

12. FORGIVENESS 135

13. ROOTS 147

14. HEALTH 159

15. SCHOOLING 171

16. CITIES 183

17. SECURITY 195

18. STRANGERS 205

19. EVERYTHING 215

ACKNOWLEDGEMENTS

We are much indebted to our wives, Auriel and Loralee, whose support has made the writing possible. We would also like to thank those whose generous financial support helped fund the writing and production of this book, and also the many others who shared with us their expertise or commented on the manuscript. Among these are: John Ashcroft, Amy Boucher Pye, Will Candler, Andrew Crook, Tom Fish (and Naomi Fish, age 10), Ian and Jane Gregg, Ann Holt, Gideon Hudson, Piers Hudson, Alison Inglis-Jones, Emma Joynson-Hicks, James Lee, Andrew Marfleet, Paul Mills, Helen Pearson, James Perry, Claire Pover, Paul Sandham, Bénédicte Scholefield and Anna Silvester. A special word of thanks is due to Marilyn Collins, who coordinated communication in the production of the manuscript, and to Nicola Morgan, who edited the text. Whatever faults remain cannot be blamed on our competent and patient advisors.

PREFACE

Ten years ago, we began to discuss a book on relationships. What finally emerged from that discussion was a book called *The R Factor* – a fairly substantial work on political economics.

What we proposed was a simple but radical idea. Society is a network of relationships, private and professional. If those relationships don't work, quality of life goes down and organisational performance suffers. Consequently, it's in everybody's interest to make sure that relationships work well.

We set out to show just how far-reaching the effects of poor relationships are, and put forward a framework for a 'relationships approach' to policy-making and management.

The book gave rise to a Cambridge-based 'think and do tank' called the Relationships Foundation. Since the publication of *The R Factor* in 1993, the Relationships Foundation has developed a number of major initiatives, showing that a 'relationships approach' is effective in policy areas as diverse as criminal justice, healthcare, and unemployment (for more information, see www.relationshipsfoundation.org).

Over the same period, relationships management has increasingly begun to drive the way both corporates and public services operate. As it becomes harder to differentiate products, so more emphasis is placed on the organisation's relationship with the customer, on productive teamwork, and on helping staff to resolve tensions between the worlds of work and life.

Against that background, it seemed natural to plan a second book, dealing with relationships as an issue of individual decision-making. Like its predecessor, *The R Option* starts from an apparently obvious premise. We all have relationships, and the quality of our relationships determines how happy and effective we are. Yet few of us give much thought to arranging our lives in a way that will make our relationships work.

The R Option is a lifestyle book of the most thorough kind. Get serious about prioritising relationships, and the consequences will soon ripple into every corner of your life. There's no prescription – just a lively discussion of the ideas and practical suggestions about how to apply them.

Writing a book of this kind, there's always a danger of appearing over-wise. We have thought through some ideas and values, and we are committed to live by them. However, neither of us will claim to be a raging success at relationships. If we'd found relationships easy, we would never have written this book.

Readers have sometimes asked us 'where we're coming from' in terms of pushing this or that agenda. Implicitly, relationships are valued in a wide variety of religious, philosophical and political movements. They are pivotal, however, in the Christian tradition, where they underlie not only ethics but a whole understanding of the nature of God. Both intellectually and personally, therefore, the book has strongly Christian roots.

There are two other points that we need to explain as an introduction to this book.

Neither 'spouse' nor 'partner' is fully satisfactory as a label for those in long-term domestic relationships. We have chosen to prefer the term 'partner' on the basis of its non-exclusivity, though, of course, many partners will be married and are more accurately described as spouses. Consequently, the term 'spouse' appears only where the context is clearly that of marriage.

Also, after we published *The R Factor,* many readers wanted to know which of us was the 'I' who addressed them in the book. The answer was sometimes one, and sometimes the other. We used the device to keep the text readable and to avoid the rather awkward alternative of sounding like identical twins. In *The R Option*, we have chosen to keep the 'I' device but have identified who is speaking in each case. We have also included biographical details about ourselves, which will tell you more about what led us to write this book on relationships and what experiences helped shape it.

Finally, if, when reading this book, you are reminded of experiences that have shaped your own relationships, if you find yourself strongly agreeing (or disagreeing) with what is said, if you feel like sharing with others what has worked for you in building your own relationships, may we invite you to share with us and other readers your views, reflections and stories? In particular, you can post messages to the discussion forum that we have set up on the Relationships Foundation's website at:

www.relationshipsfoundation.org/R_Option_discussion.html.

Do get in touch – we'd love to hear from you and learn through you!

Michael Schluter   **David John Lee**

ABOUT THE AUTHORS

MICHAEL SCHLUTER

Michael Schluter studied Economics and Economic History at Durham University. He then did a PhD in Agricultural Economics at Cornell University in the USA, which involved 18 months of field work in rural India. He lived in Kenya from 1974 to 1982, working first as a manager for a local company setting up rural industries, and then as a research fellow with the International Food Policy Research Institute and as a consultant economist with the World Bank.

He returned to England in 1982 to establish the Jubilee Centre as a Christian think-tank. In 1985, he brought together a coalition of retailers, unions, churches and other religious leaders to form the Keep Sunday Special Campaign which, in 1986, famously inflicted on Margaret Thatcher her only major defeat in the House of Commons. Following that, he helped to set up high-level meetings between the South African Establishment and the ANC between 1987 and 1991, held mainly before Nelson Mandela's release.

He is now chairman of the Relationships Foundation, a charity established in 1993 that seeks to have the importance of relationships recognised and acted upon in public life.

In addition, he is chairman of Citylife, an Industrial and Provident Society set up by the Relationships Foundation to develop innovative city-based responses to unemployment and urban regeneration.

Michael Schluter lives in Cambridge. He is married with three grown-up children and two grandchildren. In his spare time (of which he admits he has very little), he enjoys watching rugby and reading history.

Here is how Michael describes his own 'relational' journey:

I was born into a middle class family living in the South-East of England, the third child of four. My father worked at that time in the City of London as a commodity trader.

Through my teenage years, I learnt most about relationships, I suspect, from interaction with my two older sisters and younger brother. My understanding of R Options ranged from the girl down the road to one I had met last holidays. At university one of my R Options became more serious. I had a dawning realisation of the importance of friendship as I got to know the woman who became my wife. My interests were also taken up with a quest to 'change the world'. The particular part of the world which caught my imagination at that time was India; I felt overwhelmed by the immensity of its poverty and malnutrition.

Although I learnt many things in the years that followed, first in the USA and then in Indian villages studying agricultural development, a focus on relationships was not one of them. It was only when I went to live in Africa in 1974 that the significance of what I later called 'The R Factor' gradually dawned on me. I learnt this 'relational perspective' partly from the way my African friends looked at life. For instance, in a local telephone call, while I was rushing to 'do the business', they would want first to ask after my wife and children. While I was interested only in costs and levels of production at the rural factory where I worked, they were concerned about relationships with the farmers who supplied us, and the factory staff.

Later, while working for the World Bank and the International Food Policy Research Institute, on a trip to Tanzania I came up against Nyerere's version of Socialism. In economic terms it did not deliver the goods. But then the local varieties of Marxism in Ethiopia and Capitalism in Kenya seemed to have equally undesirable social consequences. Was there an alternative?

It was in reflecting on my Christian beliefs in the light of my African experience that I stumbled on the perspective that the world is primarily about the way people relate to God and to each other. Love is the dominant theme of Christianity, and love is a category of relationships. I can trace this insight to a particular day in 1981, my personal equivalent of Archimedes jumping out of his bath with the shout of 'Eureka'. My family was grateful I was not in the bath at the time! However, it was to take another 10 years to think through the implications of this simple insight.

Back in Britain with my family in 1982, I started a range of social and campaigning initiatives from the back of my house. However, it was only in retrospect in 1993 that I realised the common denominator in all these initiatives was once again the theme of relationships. The Sunday Campaign was focused around relationships within families and communities, between employers and employees, and between large retailers and small shopkeepers. Credit Action looked at relationships between lenders and borrowers, and the stress on family relationships caused by debt. And the work in South Africa was about inter-racial relationships and concerned with a peaceful transfer of power. The principle of the R Factor was staring me in the face.

But this is not the end of the story. Since setting up the Relationships Foundation I have had to take a long hard look at my own patterns of relating to those around me. When my wife became severely depressed in 1993/4, I realised I was myself largely to blame as I had been single-mindedly fighting the Sunday Campaign, while she coped with relational difficulties at work at the same time as the children were leaving home. Subsequently, as she gradually recovered and trained as a counsellor, I began to learn from her to reflect on my personal relationships at home and in the office. This has often been helpful, but also painful.

As a typical British male, I have not had much time for 'feelings'. I have needed to learn belatedly to get in touch with my emotions, to allow them to be a legitimate part of who I am and how I react to situations. There is still a long way to go. I have discovered within myself pockets of anger and resentment which it makes me blush even to mention. I have also had to learn how to get out of 'victim mode', where I blame everyone but myself for my work overload, for example, or my constant tiredness: these problems are the result of my choices, for which I have to accept responsibility.

So this book is, for me, work in progress. It is an attempt to look at the whole of life – both private life and public life – from a relational perspective. It comes out of my conviction, and my experience, that it is in and through our relationships that we discover our *true selves. Those relationships which provide our security, and form our identity, are not only those which are most intimate, in our homes and with our friends and families, but those which we experience through serendipity in our places of work, and as we mix with everyone from our GP to the shop assistant. Those like myself with a Christian faith would want to add the profound mystery of having a relationship with a personal God which gives meaning to all our other relationships.*

For all of us, each relationship, each moment of communication, is an opportunity to give as well as to receive. It is this which explains why each person, from the senior citizen to the tiny child, has such incalculable value.

I believe relationships are the most important investments we can make. They do not often give instant returns. They require patience and persistence. But, unlike financial investment, investment in relationships is not a one-off event. It is a way of life – where the returns are beyond our ability to measure.

DAVID JOHN LEE

David John Lee was born in London. After completing his BA at Oxford University, he studied at Regent College, Vancouver, and took up a career in writing and publishing.

He has written a number of books, including *Ex Machina*, a collection of Christian theatre scripts, and *Doomsday: the Survivor's Guide*, the only title released by HarperCollins UK for the Millennium.

He has wide-ranging experience in public speaking, cartooning, visual design, and publicity. His work has been staged at the Edinburgh Festival Fringe. He has also run a widely-acclaimed exhibition of work by the UK's leading advertising agencies, including Saatchi & Saatchi and Abbott Mead Vickers.

In 2001, David John Lee became Senior Writer for Haggai Institute, an international organisation promoting leadership training for evangelism.

His other interests include fossil collection and messing around with Land Rovers. He and his wife Loralee have adopted three children from India. Currently they live on the Isle of Dogs in London's Docklands.

Here is what David says about his own 'awakening' to the importance of relationships:

For many years – the first twenty-two, to be exact – I bought into the assumption that relationships just happened. I seemed to start relationships in more or less the same haphazard way I caught colds. Some people I couldn't avoid (father, mother, siblings, teachers). Most – the billions around the rest of the planet – I never met. And between these two extremes I found myself drawn to this or that individual simply because we went to the same school or shared the same hobby. In one case, a sworn enemy became a friend overnight just because I taught him how to draw battleships.

The first conscious relationship-decision I made was to marry the Canadian girl I'd met during my studies in Vancouver. 'Well, I guess we'd better get married', I told her one evening – a sadly unromantic way to begin a lifelong partnership, but consistent with my belief that relationships simply crept up on you like forgotten dental appointments on the calendar.

Once married, we really did make some choices. In appearance, at least, the first was locational: between settling in Canada and settling in the UK. We went for the latter, mainly on the grounds that my wife, though well-travelled in the Far East, had yet to experience the joys of living in what Canadians fondly call 'the Old Country'. In doing so, of course, we were making a relational choice – literally between Canadian relations and British.

We also made a choice about lifestyle – a choice in which relationships were central. Being young, and in love, and not yet in settled careers, and also rather under the influence of the sloppy countercultural values of the time, we decided to take part-time jobs in order to spend more of the day together. My newly-acquired ambition to write novels seemed to fit this plan snugly. (I hadn't yet discovered that professional writing eats up more time, and in a less predictable way, than managing a bank.) And thus my noble commitment to Art and general vow of poverty combined to put us under pressures we had neither sought nor anticipated.

Perhaps we were unusually tough, or perhaps just unusually dim, but we managed to stick this arrangement out for the best part of a decade. Looking back, I suspect that becoming bank managers would have been the smarter move. At least we'd have had the money to go on holiday.

There were compensations. I'm pretty sure I have the distinction of being the only Oxford graduate ever turned down for the position of laundry assistant at Edinburgh Psychiatric Hospital (a particularly low point, that). Lacking career paths meant we could move through an amazing variety of places, and meet a lot of different people. And although the Novel never edged Jeffrey Archer off the best-seller list (never got finished, actually), writing opened up opportunities that most bank managers never get.

One of those opportunities involved ghosting a book on the Keep Sunday Special Campaign for Michael Schluter. The following year, we collaborated on follow-up about family debt management. And finally we started mapping out the ideas that found expression in a book called The R Factor.

Researching relationships in the early 1990s allowed me to process intellectually some of the half-formed principles I'd leaned towards since I got married. What I discovered surprised me. Relationships were the girders holding up whole tower blocks of civic order, organisational success, and personal happiness. There were enormous benefits attached to 'doing relationships well' – and most of us, institutions as well as individuals, seemed to be doing them rather badly.

I was in the same mess as everyone else. Surrounded by work pressures. With not enough time. Handicapped through sheer habit. Wanting to do the best but frequently defeated by circumstance and bad luck. It gradually dawned on me that I needed to take responsibility, and take control.

I think that is one reason why this book contains so many references to decision. Some relational problems can only be tackled at an organisational level (government or company policy). But many lie in our own power to change – and in more areas of life than we generally bother to think about.

In my own case, the idea of investing in relationships took concrete form in our decision to adopt three girls from India. I've met a lot of parents for whom 'having kids' has been inevitable, like ageing. For my wife and I it was a matter of consciously opting-in. It felt a little like base jumping from a skyscraper – but I have never once regretted it.

Relationships are, I suppose, a philosophy, an approach to living. I'm not Mahatma Gandhi. My sister will tell you that she almost always has to call me, which isn't a great advertisement for someone who thinks relationships should be put first. On the other hand, there is a difference between arriving and travelling in the right direction. That is, so long as you're actually on the move.

CHAPTER ONE

RELATIONSHIPS

Last month, I (David) faced a crisis: my wife almost died. She'd gone to the emergency department on the Saturday, suffering from a mild allergy reaction. They kept her in for observation. The following evening I got a call from the intensive care unit, asking me to come in quickly. They'd discovered double pneumonia. Her allergies were preventing the use of the necessary antibiotics. They'd sedated and paralysed her, and put her on a ventilator to force oxygen into her lungs. 'Come quickly' meant 'Be ready for the worst'.

Initially, of course, you don't believe it. How can someone you shared dinner with the night before be at the point of death? How can this clever, attractive, articulate woman be lying here, kept breathing by machines? And then you become suddenly, vividly aware of the future. The emptiness. The children in the waiting room who think Mummy's coming home tomorrow. All the horrid, messy complications of life taking a lurch onto the dark side.

There was nothing we could do. I took the children home, put them to bed, and began what, I can truthfully say, was the worst night of my life, praying that the phone would not ring.

It would be fatuous to draw from this situation the moral that 'relationships matter'. Of course they matter. We all know they matter. Relationships – with family, friends, colleagues and community – matter in the way that health matters: as a precondition of wellbeing. Something you take for granted when you have it, and miss desperately when it's gone.

But the idea that 'relationships matter' has fairly shallow roots in the culture we live in. The word *love* crops up a lot, and feel-good stories of friends enjoying good times together will often draw high ratings in the media. But strip this away, and you find that many of the hard economic and cultural drivers are pushing in a different direction.

Underlying our banking, borrowing, spending and paying of taxes has emerged the unspoken assumption that we function, first and foremost, as *individuals.* 'Relationship' is a state we may choose to enter into, and choose to withdraw from. Where relationships exist – personal or contractual – we find it increasingly easy to think in terms of what others owe to us rather than what we owe to others. We have rights. We have freedom of choice. And we have possessions (income, house, clothing, car, holiday destination) from which we derive a sense of status and by means of which we signal who we are.

All this is the stuff of our everyday life. And the mood of it is defensive rather than open, about protecting ourselves from others rather than entering into creative co-operation with them. We teach our children the street-fighting skills of passing examinations, competing for jobs and getting ahead in a career. We don't often pass down to them the relational wealth of valuing and actively cultivating good relationships.

RELATIONSHIPS AS A PRINCIPLE OF LIFE

Why do we not use relationships as a way of ordering and prioritising our actions, in the same way as we use the environment, or health, or money?

Over the last twenty years, the welfare of the planet has come to influence our day-to-day decisions on the products we buy (everything from fuel to toilet paper) and has turned up as an option on the election ballot paper. Many of our so-called 'lifestyle' choices have to do with levels of saturated fat in foods and the ability of various exercise products to keep us fit. Similarly, it's second nature to us to select options (for homes, cameras, mobile phones) on the basis of how much they cost.

The main assertion of this book is that relationships can be treated in exactly this manner. Further, that prioritising 'good relationships' in the way we live is more fundamental, more far-reaching, and more beneficial than prioritising the environment, health, or money.

Relationships, after all, are just so basic to everything we do, both as individuals and as a society.

For example:

1. Relationships are the key to self-understanding

A little girl doing biology homework asked, 'Mummy, where did I come from?' Embarrassed, her mother replied, 'From under a gooseberry bush.' Later, the little girl went to ask her granny, 'Where did Mummy come from?' The grandmother replied, 'A stork brought her.' The girl wrote in her homework book: 'We haven't had a normal birth in our family for three generations.'

Relationships answer our need to understand where we come from and who we are. According to J.H. Oldham:

> *It is through our responses to other persons that we become persons. It is others who challenge, enlighten and enrich us. There is no such thing as the isolated individual ... Reality is the lived relation. Through sharing in the giving and receiving of mutual being the 'I' becomes real. Reality is an activity in which I share without being able to appropriate it for myself. Where there is no sharing there is no reality. Where there is appropriation by the self there is no reality ... all real life is meeting.*[1]

As we talk to other people, we learn to put our own experience of life into a wider perspective. We see in others the faults most prevalent in ourselves, and we see what we are especially gifted at and thus what we can contribute to society. We learn the need for interdependence, and that no one is economically or psychologically self-sufficient. We learn that, just as trees are more than just timber, people are more than just 'human resources'.

2. Relationships are the key to happiness, reputation and self-esteem

Day after day, the quality of your relationships impacts on the quality of your life. *Relational* events – a disagreement with the boss, a successful negotiation, a great evening out with friends, a week when grown-up children don't call – will ripple out, deeply affecting your confidence, concentration, work performance, and sense of wellbeing. Quite obviously – from a personal as well as a business point of view – there's a big pay-off to getting 'relationship management' right.

We are happiest when we know we are loved. Growing up amid supportive and positive relationships, we develop self-esteem. Without those close relationships, you can lose your sense of personal security and wellbeing. Even fame and wealth are no substitutes. The comedian Tony Hancock, like many before and after him, was driven to suicide in large measure because he felt lonely and misunderstood.

Good personal relationships distinguish the impression you leave behind in this world. It was said that the pollster George Gallup had written on his tombstone, '84 per cent of people think I have gone to heaven.' It's more likely someone will be remembered as 'A beloved son and father' than as 'The executive who restructured his company three times in five years and thus sustained shareholder value through a difficult period in the markets'.

3. Relationships are the key to re-establishing the balance in our personal lives

Western cultures tend to muddle money and relationships. A market-driven culture keeps telling us the bottom line is financial. We all have to pay the rent. And most of the opportunities on offer – to travel, dress well, live in pleasant surroundings – have to be bought.

But we also know that, when relationships go wrong, money is almost useless. Money itself is only a way of tallying how much one person can ask of another. As anyone in business knows, you can't even make money without effective relationships, because markets and companies are, in the end, only groups of people working together.

The problem is that we can find ourselves so driven by financial imperatives that we feel 'life is passing us by'. The full life, the well-rounded life, isn't the privilege of the wealthy few. It is reached by committing yourself to relationship goals alongside the financial ones.

4. Relationships are the key to social support

Thankfully, when my wife was ill, the dreaded midnight phone call never came. The first call came the next morning. And it wasn't the hospital, but an American colleague I'd emailed the previous evening. He was the first of many – family members, colleagues and friends – who'd got wind of what was going on, and phoned or emailed to offer me help and support.

Almost certainly, anyone reading this book will have had a similar experience. One of the reasons we need friends and family is simply that we all need help – emotional and practical.

WHAT THIS BOOK DOES

This book is about looking at life 'relationally' – that is, in terms of the impact of your personal lifestyle decisions on your relationships with your friends, family, colleagues and community. The relational way of looking at life is far-reaching. When you stop to think about it, almost every decision you make has significant relationship implications.

More than once in the book, we've used the phrase 'self-management'. That's about the measure of it. There are no one-dimensional fixes for lifestyle in and around the busy professional and corporate world. It's not like a toothache you take to a dentist and then forget about. It's a process of constant choosing, which affects everything from your investments to your sexuality.

The phrase 'self-management' shouldn't be taken to mean that relationships are merely an instrument for achieving personal satisfaction. To be concerned about a relationship is to be concerned about the person on the other end of it, and to discover the irony – no doubt familiar – that fulfilment comes through putting the other person's interests first.

Ultimately, the question you're settling is what kind of life you want. When my wife got out of hospital ten days later, we spent a long time discussing exactly that, against the background of a busy, professional household. That's where I happen to be right now. But you may be asking the same question, whether you're single, or retired, or separated, or a lone parent, or in a partnership without children, and no matter what your colour, gender or sexual orientation.

Finally, note that this book interfaces with, and is based on, a much broader body of research into the way public policy impacts on the way we relate, and how the way we relate impacts on public policy. If you are interested in this, as well as the approach outlined in this book, you will find details on our website (www.relationshipsfoundation.org).

---

1 Oldham, J.H., *Real Life in Meeting* (London: Sheldon Press, 1958).

CHAPTER TWO

TIME

I (Michael) was about to board a flight to Geneva recently when I realised I'd lost something important. I patted my pockets, turned out my hand luggage, patted my pockets again, then fought my way through to the steward at the boarding gate.

'Look, I think I left my phone at the security check. Do I have time to go back?'

She eyed the clock. 'The plane's leaving in twenty minutes.'

'I'll take the train back to the terminal.'

'You're not allowed to take the train back', she said. 'The train only carries passengers one way. I can call the security check if you want.'

She picked up the receiver on her desk.

I tapped my foot impatiently. How could I have lost a mobile phone? I'd arrived at the airport with the device jammed between my shoulder and my jaw, trying to squeeze in all those crucial calls before I left the country. I'd had it with me as I got my foreign exchange, and bought some last-minute health insurance. Then I put it down to go through the metal detector – and just left it behind.

'What make is it?' asked the steward.

'A Motorola.'

'They have it. If you want, they can send it to Lost and Found.'

For a moment, my hopes rose. 'Where's that?'

'At the other end of the airport.'

I thanked her, and went back to my seat, feeling dejected.

But at least the phone hadn't been stolen. Really, all I had to do was contact my secretary and arrange for it to be returned to my office before I got back. I still had fifteen minutes left. Instinctively, I reached into my pocket to make the call – then realised there was nothing there.

THE TIME PROBLEM

When we say that the 'pace' of life is increasing, we don't necessarily mean there are more things to do. Statutory working hours have changed relatively little in the last thirty years. A lot of people are better off, and have more labour-saving devices sitting around in the home. On that basis, life should be growing more leisurely.

But time has become a problem because daily living now requires us to manage many more *relationships.* In the couple of hours before I boarded the plane to Geneva, I made phone calls to ten different people. I changed money with an eleventh person. I bought insurance from a twelfth. Left my phone with a thirteenth. Sought assistance from a fourteenth. And all I was doing was going on holiday for a week.

In part, the problem results simply from having greater access to people. We do a lot more travelling and commuting. And the increasing finesse of communications technology – mobiles, text-messaging, email – puts literally millions of people at our fingertips (and us at theirs), at very low cost.

Perversely, of course, the expansion of these new technologies immediately upgrades our expectations of each other.

Now that I (Michael) can afford to call Kenya, my mother in Nairobi would think me negligent if I didn't ring several times a month for a chat. Similarly, in business, the ability to reach people results in more colleagues being consulted in decision-making, in more referring back to base by negotiators, and in more shopping around for the best deal.

On top of all that, there is the sheer complexity of being a choice-making consumer. The more goods you own, and the more services you tap into, the more relationships are involved in your day-to-day life management.

When my (David's) computer died recently, almost a whole working day got used up in contacting two technical helplines, driving to the store to buy a new part, and finally delivering the machine – still dead – to a repair workshop.

And we have a lot more going on in our lives than computers. We have cars, homes, insurance, groceries, banks, investments, home improvements, electricity, vacations, videos, income tax, clothes, ticket cancellations, schooling, health, and – in my case – an infestation of ants in the kitchen.

All these things, and more, connect you to different groups of people, requiring you to make visits, send letters, make choices, use the phone. You might argue that technology makes the contact easier, and to an extent that is true. But technology also adds a new layer of frustration, creating lengthy call centre queues, and absurdities like the phone bill I (David) received this morning for £00.09p (that's 8p in calls and 1p tax) – for which I nonetheless had to write a cheque, address an envelope, and find a stamp.[1]

TIME AND RELATIONSHIPS

Being so deeply connected to so many other people would be fine if only we had a couple of extra days in the week. But relationships don't compress to fit schedules. A five-minute exchange with your phone banking operative may be perfectly satisfactory. But on-going relationship management needs time. You can't create relationships instantly any more than you can create an instant, well-matured claret.

A sad but true story: a married couple with high-paying jobs based in different parts of Europe have so little time together that they are seeking to have a baby by IVF. In other words, it seems that the woman has more opportunity to get to a local fertility clinic than to get into bed with her partner.

In the end, there is no substitute for *quantity time.* You need it to build relationships, and you need it to maintain relationships. Beyond a certain point, prolonged and repeated absence from a partner will tend to corrode intimacy.

To an extent, this is because separations make people more used to coping on their own. While one partner flies off to a conference in Dubai, the other may be bearing the brunt of routine life-maintenance – teen-managing, shopping, and getting the car fixed.

It's also because keeping a relationship in good condition takes regular input. Home partnerships start failing their health checks long before they get dragged into intensive care. The qualities that keep a partnership in shape – things like mutual support, listening, trust, working through problems, and good sex – all require the commitment of serious time.

In this sense, you could look on your relationships as a kind of *wealth* – an intangible and finite asset that shapes who you are and determines, to a massive extent, what quality of life you will have.

For example, like money, this wealth is something you may inherit. Children can come into families that are *relationally rich*, or into families that are *relationally poor*. Research shows that relational poverty, not just financial hardship, accounts for divorcees' children being at higher risk of mental illness, of showing aggressive or withdrawn behaviour, and of being more likely to underachieve academically and end up unemployed.[2] This doesn't mean all children of divorcees suffer these consequences. But the nature of your past relationships does much to make you what you are today.[3]

Second, relational wealth, not material wealth, plays the greatest part in producing personal happiness and support. When you want advice and encouragement, you look to your relationships. When you want a good time, you look to your relationships. Friends and loved ones are your main protection when you're ill, bereaved, unemployed, or depressed. It's there you find respect, love and commitment. By contrast, poverty in relationships – social isolation, lack of social skills, relationships crashing – severely reduces your quality of life and increases your susceptibility to illness.

Not surprisingly, there is a connection between relational poverty and the time-counting culture of the West.

One thing that struck me (Michael) forcibly during years spent in Africa was that, despite the crises of poverty, war and famine, ordinary people in Africa are often far more cheerful than ordinary people in Britain and the USA. Childbirth and bereavement have the same emotional impact everywhere. But the inherited relational wealth in most African countries is far greater than ours. If there were such an index as GRP – Gross Relational Product – it's sobering to think that Britain and America would probably rank among the world's poorest nations.

Robert Putnam put the point well with reference to the United States, in a recent issue of *Le Monde*:

> *The problem is that Americans are so hard working they no longer have free time in which to see one another. The amount*

*of time friends spend at each other's houses has dropped 35
per cent since the Seventies while, at home, families are a
third less likely to eat together. There is also far less participation in civic affairs: over the past 30 years, the time Americans
devote to supporting a political party has halved ... In terms of
social capital, America has become truly impoverished.*[4]

DO WE VALUE WORK TOO MUCH?

When I (David) was small, I used to ask my father what he did when
he went to work. Other people's dads would say things like 'I repair
televisions' or 'I design houses'. Not mine. 'I have this big machine
on my desk', he'd reply, feigning a twinge in his back. 'And every day
I have to sit there and w-i-i-i-ind the handle to make the pennies
come out ...'

I can't remember now whether I believed this story or not. Today,
it can be argued, the workplace has become 'newly hospitable to
sociability' in the sense that long working hours make it an important
arena for friendship.[5] But it is still the *work*place – the place you go
because you need to swap some of your time for money.

When we talk about the work–life 'crisis' we usually mean that this
'money' side of life is getting more than its fair share of our time and
attention. Fear of redundancy keeps us winding that handle. Or the
need for promotion. Or perhaps a desire not to let the side down by
looking like a slacker.[6]

Clearly, though, the boundary between life and work is a good deal
more fluid than that. The people we work with, and the people we
know outside the workplace, can both provide us with crucial social
support. Work is as much a 'people' or 'relationship' environment as
life is. It's just a different set of relationships.

These relationship networks can extend a long way. There are your
bosses and immediate colleagues, then other employees, customers,
suppliers, financial backers, shareholders, members of the surrounding community, even the staff in the bistro where you buy your lunch.
Everyone who affects the organisation, or is affected by it, belongs in
some way to its network.

These relationships can be positive and supportive even when you're under pressure. Stay late to conclude that all-important deal, for example, and everyone will thank you. The boss's figures look better; the directors can turn in a glowing quarterly report; shareholders get dividends; customers get faster service and perhaps lower prices. You get approval and a sense of achievement, and your boosted confidence feeds back further into the general creative synergy.

Getting workplace relationships right is a priority some employers take seriously. William Sieghart is proprietor of the London-based Forward Publishing. 'My philosophy', he told the Financial Times recently, 'is about enabling people to do brilliant work. If I can get the atmosphere and the support right, they'll do that.'

The support includes free monthly massage, yoga classes, and an obligatory three-month sabbatical every six years. How much time his people spend at work isn't the major issue. 'We all know', says Sieghart, 'that you can get more work done in four days than five if you put your mind to it.'[7]

By the same token, distant, or time-poor relationships can carry high costs. You don't need much savvy to see that bad relationships in any organisation spell inefficiency and performance decline, as well as a lot of stress for those involved. Not surprisingly, management guru Tom Peters concludes that 'Today's wisest firms ... are those that are tops at consciously investing in relationships.'[8]

TAKING THE R OPTION WITH TIME

Western newspapers constantly run articles on the 'work–life balance'. But the term is misleading. The real issue isn't stopping work taking over your life. Nor is the choice between earning money at work and having relationships at home. It's managing the whole range of your relationships – in work and outside work – in a way that maximises outcomes.

Usually, you will sense the need to put time and energy into selected and significant relationships. But time pressure, resulting in part from developments in new technologies and an increase in the total number of your relationships, means that the amount of time you can give to each one goes down.

This impacts on you in two ways. First, it puts all your relationships into competition. Work colleagues, clients, friends and family compete for the same scarce commodity – your time. Consequently, transactions may have to be conducted at high speed (with your line manager, for example, or your GP, or your children's teacher, or even the homeless person you step over as you leave the station).

Second, it places particular pressure on your central, supportive relationships – ones with friends and family that often lie outside the workplace, and that can't be maintained adequately by sending an email every other day.[9]

Clearly, one solution to the time problem is to simplify your life. I (Michael) have a friend who gave up a top job in the private sector to go and live in a small village in Scotland. In effect, this was rather like becoming a monk. It increased the time available for significant relationships by reducing the number of relationships he had to be involved in.

This is one way out of the dilemma. But you take it at the cost of opting out of the mainstream where the decisions are made that influence the way we're going to live. The world has changed, and will continue to change. Mobility and telecommunications are the new realities. If we value relationships, we have to find ways of making them work effectively within these new constraints.

In particular, to tackle the tension between time and relationships, you may like to consider these ways of applying the R option.

1. Look at what your employer can do to help

It's worth talking with the personnel office to find out what options are open. For example, how much room is there for flexitime? What precedents have been set in this area? When does the employer really need you to be there, and when could you work just as effectively from home?[10] Is a four-day week an option?

Flexible working arrangements – including flexitime, part-time work, job-sharing, shift-swapping, working from home, and team-based self-rostering – are increasingly being considered as options by employers seeking to attract and retain quality staff.[11]

An investment banker in the City of London recently agreed with his boss to work nine out of ten working days in every fortnight, thus freeing up every second Friday to walk his children to school and spend the day with his wife. A small change – with big benefits.

Similarly, a woman in senior management at a large UK charitable organisation uses the existing flexibility on hours to work longer Monday to Thursday so she can take off Friday afternoons and extend her weekend.

It may be possible to adjust your responsibilities, transfer to a different job in the firm, or reach some other working arrangement. But don't be afraid to be frank, and thrash it out. A good employer will always listen. After all, it's in the firm's interests to attract and retain quality staff, and to avoid the costs of recruitment and retraining that result from high staff turnover. Also, contented employees usually do a better job.

2. Give value for money in the hours you do

At the Relationships Foundation, I (Michael) had one particular manager who never failed to leave the office at exactly five o'clock. Day in, day out, he was out of the door at five. As an employer, I might have concluded that he was more concerned about catching his train than about getting the job done. In fact, though, the thought never crossed my mind – because I knew that during office hours he gave himself to the job 150 per cent.

Partly this is an efficiency issue. According to the *Financial Times,* half of middle managers say that long hours are caused more by inefficiency than by workload. Most would prefer to work longer days in a four-day week.[12]

Pulling your weight counts for a lot in work relationships. Win your employer's respect by your focus and efficiency, and you're likely to find it much easier to get away on time. Being sloppy, starting late, making use of the firm's phone and email in the firm's time – these things not only undermine an employer's confidence in you, but also prevent you reaching the end of your checklist by close of play.

Of course, not all employees can avoid their work spilling over. A dealer on the Stock Market can't leave work at five without missing the afternoon's trading in New York. But where your job allows you to pack your working time more tightly, it's often worth doing it.

3. Don't underestimate the value of 'chatting time' at work

Of course, if you are young and not particularly attached, your ability and willingness to soak up extra work time may be proportionately greater. More than that, you may have a good deal of your social life invested in the workplace. You may share projects with colleagues, share recreational time at facilities – like bars, clubs, or gyms – that are close to the office, even go home to shared accommodation. In that case, a good deal of blurring happens around the work–life boundary, and 'overworking' may be both exhilarating and socially rewarding.

Even if you have family responsibilities, work remains an important social environment. After all, you spend a substantial amount of time with your colleagues. And from an employer's point of view, it's worth remembering that 'relational space' in the workplace constitutes a real asset. As Professor Clive Holtham of London City University admitted recently: 'People are saying to me that the most important technology for knowledge-sharing is the coffee machine.'[13]

4. Use your travel time effectively

A similar point can be made about journeys to work. The average worker in the UK commutes almost 3,000 miles per year.[14] The obvious option here is to locate in a place that reduces your commuting time – though, as you can see from the chapter on roots, this may have unforeseen consequences.

But there are other issues. Running a second car, for instance, may save you twenty minutes a day in journey time to the station. But that second car has to be fuelled, washed, and maintained – a cost estimated at around 23p (35¢) per mile.[15] And losing the twenty minutes' exercise involved in walking may force you to put time aside elsewhere simply to keep fit.

Similarly, you may not save as much time as you think by taking the plane. Flying from London to Edinburgh takes little more than an hour. But by the time you've embarked and disembarked, and travelled to and from airports, flying turns out to be little faster than taking the train. Plus, the train will usually give you a long stretch of undisturbed work time.

If you absolutely have to travel by car, there are relational as well as financial reasons for car-sharing. The Internet has made it increasingly easy to find other people in your postcode area who are travelling in the same direction.[16]

5. If you've got children, face up to the consequences

One argument often wheeled out for staying late, winding the handle, and turning out the pennies is that quality relationships need money.

There is a lot of truth in this. Poverty is miserable, and is a proven ingredient in failed marriages and partnerships. Put the other way: as already noted, overtime at work can underwrite intrinsically life-restoring things like a good holiday.

But it's easy to get sloppy with this argument – especially if relationships at home are going through a rough patch. If you anticipate grief when you step in the door, you'll find it that much easier to stay on at work. And, of course, as supplier of that vital cash you have a cast-iron excuse.

Similarly, a lot of busy middle-income parents try to ring-fence the time they spend in direct, hands-on child-rearing. Unfortunately, research evidence simply does not support the pious hope that 'quantity time' taken away from kids can be compensated for by short, high-velocity 'quality time;' by handing out Gameboys and mobile phones; or by professional caring.[17]

In the end there's just no substitute for 'being there' on a pretty regular basis. And the older a child gets, the less discretion you have in setting the timetable. If you're not available the moment your 16-year-old wants to unload on you, the opportunity for that all-important parent–child heart-to-heart chat could be gone for ever.

In the final analysis, almost any work assignment can be done by somebody else, and to that extent, very few people in the workplace can truly be called indispensable. But nobody else fully substitutes for you in your role as parent. If you're not there, it's going to get noticed.

6. Ensure as far as possible that time off coincides

Shared time off has taken a hammering recently – particularly in the UK. Christmas remains almost sacrosanct as family time. But Sunday as a joint recreation day is much less universal than it was. For many in retail and related professions, market pressure to relax restraints on Sunday trading has made it increasingly difficult to spend shared time with others.

Contrary to popular belief, this problem doesn't affect only families and shopworkers. Your Sunday morning five-a-side football will be disrupted by weekend working. And this is now just as likely to happen to lawyers, accountants, librarians and health professionals.[18]

Flexible work arrangements widen your options for taking time off in synch. Of course, it takes extra effort and co-ordination – especially where you're also juggling school schedules – but the opportunity is there. It's a matter of taking all the variables into account, including statutory holiday time and constraints on a partner's leave, as well as the inconvenience you may cause to work colleagues by asking them to cover for you.

---

1   For American readers, the total bill was a little over a dime.
2   See, for example, *Experiments in Living: The Fatherless Father*, by Rebecca O'Neill (Civitas, September 2002), available at www.civitas.org.uk. Also Michael Argyle's excellent summary, 'The effects of relationships on wellbeing,' in Nicola Baker (ed), *Building a Relational Society* (Aldershot: Arena, 1996), p.43.
3   The impact of relationships on personality formation has long been accepted by psychiatrists. See Henry Stack Sullivan, *The Interpersonal Theory of Psychiatry,* edited by H.S. Perry and M. L. Gawel (New York: Norton, 1953).
4   Quoted in *The Week*, 9 December 2000, p.12.
5   See Arlie Bussell Hochschild, *The Time Bind* (Second Owl Books, 2001), p.46.
6   Long hours are more common in the UK than elsewhere in Europe. Average hours worked by full-time male employees in the UK is 45 hours (female employees 41). 51% work over 40 hours, and 21% work over 48 hours. In Germany, men work 41 hours and women 39. Only 12% work over 40 hours, and only 7% over 48. Source: Eurostat 2000.
7   See *Financial Times*, 8 May 2000, p. 35, 'Leadership by example not rhetoric'.
8   Tom Peters, *Liberation Management: necessary disorganisation for the nanosecond nineties,* (London: Macmillan, 1992), p.366.
9   According to an IPD survey, 'Two-fifths [of respondents] report that working long hours has resulted in arguments with their spouse or partner ... Nearly a third admit that work-related tiredness is causing their sex life to suffer, and 42% say that friendships have been damaged.' *Guardian,* 5 March 2001.
10 According to Social Trends 2001, p.83, there are now 1.6 million teleworkers in the UK (Social Trends no.31, London: Office for National Statistics).
11 In many sectors, good employees are scarcer than jobs. Among America's top employers, for example, 83% offer bounties to employees for recommending new

hires. See Robert Levering and Milton Moskowitz, 'America's Top Employers' in *Fortune,* 8 January 2001.

12 See *Financial Times*, 8 May 2000, p.34, 'The strains of juggling home and work'.

13 See *Financial Times*, 1 December 1999, IT Review, p.3.

14 See Rachel Baird, 'Lift-share scheme seeks to cut the cost of motoring' in *Express On Sunday,* 10 January 1999.

15 Source: www.nationalcarshare.co.uk

16 Nationalcarshare provide such a service – see above website address.

17 Note, for instance, that in the UK one in five children now suffers stress-related illnesses which are linked to the long hours worked by their parents (*Guardian,* 17 April 2000).

18 The UK is far ahead of its European partners in encouraging Sunday working. 39% of UK employees did Sunday work in 1999. This contrasts with 23% in Germany, 25% in France, and 15% in Spain. Source: Eurostat 2000.

CHAPTER THREE

COMMUNICATIONS

The author Howard Rheingold recently went to visit the Amish community of Pennsylvania, USA. Brought to the world's attention in the Harrison Ford film *Witness*, the Amish originally came to North America in 1710. Three hundred years later their way of life has changed little. Most still wear traditional, homespun clothes, shun the national grid, and ride around in a horse and buggy. To Rheingold, a self-confessed technophile, a trip to Amish country was surely going to feel like a visit to the dark ages.

But what he found surprised him. In fact the Amish *did* use new technologies – but only to the extent that those technologies advanced the goals of the community. When Rheingold tried to call an Amish contact, for example, he found he could only leave a phone message asking to be called back.

> *I left a message on his phone, which I later learned was located in a shanty in his neighbour's pasture. I couldn't help thinking it was awfully complicated to have a phone you used only for calling back – from a booth in a meadow. Why not make life easier and just put one in the house? 'What would that do?' another Amish man asked me. 'We don't want to be the kind of people who will interrupt a conversation at home to answer a telephone. It's not just how you use the technology that concerns us. We're also concerned about what kind of person you become when you use it.'[1]*

On this basis, the Amish have adopted a collection of modern consumer technologies ranging from disposable nappies to in-line skates and gas barbecue grills. This is not, as might appear, a gradual caving in to the realities of twenty-first century living. Rheingold concludes:

Far from knee-jerk technophobes, these are very adaptive tech-no-selectives ... the Amish have an elaborate system by which they evaluate the tools they use; their tentative, at times reluc-tant use of technology is more complex than a simple rejection or a whole-hearted embrace. What if modern Americans could agree upon criteria for acceptance, as the Amish have? Might we find better ways to wield technological power, other than simply unleashing it and seeing what happens? What can we learn from a culture that habitually negotiates the rules for new tools?

In fact, negotiating rules on technology is something Western societies do all the time. Just look at recent debates over GM foods, or the laws limiting the use of firearms. Whenever a technology threatens safety, we quickly begin negotiating rules for its use.

What we *don't* do so much is look at the effects of technology on relationships. And nowhere is this more true than in the burgeoning technology of communications.

Some concern has been expressed about mobile phones, in connection with microwave emissions. And there is an on-going argument about the policing of the Internet – so far a rather fruitless one, since the problems of legislating for such a vast transnational network are dauntingly large.

For the most part, though, we feel that technologies extending and broadening communication must be, almost inherently, good. They let us communicate more quickly, more conveniently, and at lower cost. And thus our decisions to purchase this or that mobile phone or software package come down mainly to things like price, capability, ease of use, and value as a fashion accessory.

THE HISTORY OF BEING THERE WHEN YOU'RE NOT

The shift to a 'wired world' truly deserves the title *revolution*. Its impact will be just as profound as the Agrarian and Industrial Revolutions – and it is happening much more quickly.[2]

For most of human history, instant communication has largely depended on the receiver being able to see or hear the sender. You beat drums, rang bells, lit fires, sent smoke signals. Nothing more complex could be communicated without a person going along to carry or repeat the message. Hence the origins of the marathon in Phidippides' legendary sprint to tell Athens that their army had trounced the Persians.

It wasn't until 1844, when Samuel Morse sent his groundbreaking four-word message from Baltimore to Washington,[3] that it first became possible to talk to another person *without actually being there.*

Just how far we've gone since then is illustrated by a man seen in a supermarket. He was pushing a trolley around with a phone clamped to his ear, while his partner – presumably inspecting the kitchen cupboards at home – told him what to get.

It's not hard to foresee how the various strands of modern telecommunications – mobile phone, email, text messaging – will converge in a technology that lets us talk to pretty much anyone from pretty much anywhere at pretty much any time – with no regard at all for physical location. It will be like having the whole human race in the same room.

'Unleashing it and seeing what happens' describes fairly accurately what is now going on with communications technology. Inevitably, this seismic shift in the way we communicate will affect the way we relate. But how?

REPORTS FROM WHERE WE'RE GOING

In 1998, Dr. Jan Lueck delivered a lecture to a Congressional Seminar entitled: Technology and Social Change: The Effects on Family and Community.[4] As Associate Professor of Anthropology at San José State University, she is heavily involved in the Silicon Valley Cultures Project – an on-going anthropological study of the world of professional high-tech.

Silicon Valley stands – more than any other place – at the leading edge of our dealings with communications technology. And Dr. Lueck's interest is precisely in what this technology, so readily adopted in California, is doing to everyday life. She paints this picture of a typical administrative assistant:

Sharon checks her E-mail and voice mail in the predawn hours before her children wake to prepare for any tasks that may need to be addressed immediately. She carries a pager and a cell phone so that she can stay in contact with her teenage children after they come home from school. All of them feel much safer for the presence of these devices. They can now stay out longer and be more independent since they are 'in contact'. The only time they have been physically together in several weeks is for the anthropologist's visit to their home for an interview.

One developing trend, then, appears to be that technology increases the amount of time individuals spend on their own programmes and pursuits. Since they can so easily 'touch base' with one another by phone, they feel less need to be in one place together at one time.

Linked to this is another trend – the increasing speed and fluidity of social arrangements between household members. Time is micromanaged in an exercise of precise and perpetual long-distance teamwork:

Pagers, cell phones and answering machines, and now palm pilots, are used in tandem to co-ordinate complex household schedules. Work, school and recreational activities demand transportation, sequencing and division of labour....The perceived safety net of technology also allows planning to become ever more 'just-in-time'. Message machines and pagers allow plans to be created, shifted and co-ordinated in the space of a single afternoon.

This fast-track activity depends on the lines of communication remaining open, and, not surprisingly, tempers can fray when someone drops the ball. Thus, one female partner explains, 'I get stressed when David doesn't have his phone on. You know, we have them for a reason, and I'll be trying to call him and I found out that he has the damn thing turned off.'

MOBILE PHONES FOR MOBILE RELATIONSHIPS

The advantage of the mobile is being reachable – at least in theory – everywhere and all of the time. As a time-management tool, therefore, it is second to none. If you're going to be late for an appointment, you can call ahead and save the person you're meeting a valuable thirty minutes. If your teenage daughter gets stranded at two in the morning, she can call and ask you for a lift. And if you're waiting at a station with nothing to do – then, armed with a mobile, you can make those personal calls to family that otherwise would have dropped off the end of your daily to-do list.

But of course this versatility is, by the same token, the mobile's disadvantage. Unless you take a positive decision to divert calls, conversations with important people are apt to be interrupted by less important people who want two minutes of your time. For some reason – perhaps the fear of stacking up too many voicemail messages – we feel under pressure to stay reachable.

There is also the matter of interaction quality. Mobile conversations tend to be brief, disjointed and fragmented. They suit co-ordinating and information-gathering exchanges. But hurried on-the-move chat is less useful for forming and sustaining close relationships. So issues arise over how much time in a relationship we devote to mobile interaction, and how much we reserve for non-task-oriented, uninterrupted, face-to-face relating.

Often, it's the people at the centre of the telecommunications storm who take its effects most seriously. According to the *New York Times,* 'Microsoft researcher Linda Stone warned that we now live in an age of "continuous partial attention". Cell phones and bleepers mean that we are permanently available, but in a state of constant distraction.'[5]

EMAIL AND THE LEWINSKI CONNECTION

Similarly, the difficulties rooted in the need to squeeze relationships through the narrow aperture of a given technology also crop up with email.

Like letter writing, email has to do without subliminal communication through facial expression or tone of voice. Unlike letter writing, however, it does not have a centuries-old etiquette enabling us to interpret mood, tone, and intent.

The average email is short (making it liable to be abrupt). It is instantly answerable (meaning we're more likely to dash off a reply without thinking what we're saying). And it has not inherited from letter writing the formalities of politeness (meaning we may fail to signal due respect for the recipient).[6]

In business, much attention has been paid to flame-mail – the predominantly male practice of sending abusive or insulting email messages. Email's screen-to-screen directness and lack of face-to-face contact make it easy to abuse. Even well-intentioned criticism can seem bracingly blunt. And the speed of the system causes retaliation to escalate fast. One in seventy respondents to a recent survey claimed that flame-mail had forced them to leave jobs.[7]

But the presence of email – as well as the sheer volume of communication it generates – is changing the relational environment of offices in more fundamental ways.

The ease with which information can be copied and sent leads to email overload – people receiving material they don't need but still have to process through their inbox. The effect is only made worse by email's ability to zip across departmental and international boundaries. It's not unusual in management to get over 100 emails a day. At an average two minutes each to read and reply, it will take over three hours to deal with them.

The use of email tends to limit opportunities for informal discussion that normally occur before meetings, on the phone, or in the corridor. The frequent result: increase in isolation and pressure, loss of motivation, and a cost to the sense of mutual trust and camaraderie that keeps a workplace productive. A friend working for a leading financial services company told me (Michael) that, to save time and physical effort, he would often email his secretary – even though she worked just outside the door of his office. To compensate for the lack of personal contact, he finds he has to walk round once every day to meet his team face-to-face.

Send a swift and poorly-thought-out email, and you will start a ping-pong game of requests for clarification. This could be avoided with a phone call. But in a busy office, replying to an email often substitutes for dealing with the issue. It's an example of 'not on my desk' syndrome – and the effect is that email volume, and stress, both go up.

If all that isn't sufficient cause for care, remember that deleted email saved on corporate backup tapes is now being drawn into litigation. In the recent Microsoft trial, most of the 3,000 exhibits were emails. And much of the dirt dished out on President Clinton over the Monica Lewinski scandal was recovered from the hard disk of a home PC.

THE INTERNET: THE NEW WILD FRONTIER

In contrast to email and mobile phones, communication on the Internet seems at first to be fairly one-sided.

Much of the net operates like a vast and cleverly-indexed encyclopaedia – easy to access and (because it requires no paper) easy on the world's trees. The term 'interactive' denotes only the on-screen equivalent of a menu-driven telephone information service, generating the same frustration for users who want to interact with another human being rather than with a list of Frequently Asked Questions.

But the Internet also provides a platform for a form of personal interaction. In a chat room, for instance, you can have a text-based, real-time conversation with anyone else logged on to the same virtual space. It's a system of instant messaging, like passing handwritten notes underneath a locked soundproof door.

Clearly, the potential for networking over shared interests is huge. And there is some evidence suggesting that relationships started this way can develop further. In the UK, 60–70 per cent of net users claim that they have formed some kind of online relationship, a few of which are said to have developed into either marriage or cohabiting.[8]

But, as with television, the solitary nature of Internet usage has an impact on a user's relationships. According to a recent American study of 169 people in 73 households, 'Greater use of the Internet was associated with declines in participants' communication with family members in the household, declines in the size of their social circle, and increases in their depression and loneliness.' The report concludes: 'Perhaps, by using the Internet, people are substituting poorer quality social relationships for better relationships, that is, substituting weak ties for strong ones.'[9]

In addition, as a relational environment, the Internet has some strange qualities. Once you're in a chat room, the only things other members know about you are the things you choose to disclose. And, of course, you are quite free to fib. A woman can pretend to be a man, an old person pretend to be a teenager, a white person pretend to be black – or vice versa. Harmless role-playing – or sinister self-concealment? Either way, the limitations of cyber-based relationships are fairly clear.

There is also the matter of just who you're relating to out there. The Cyberangels, an offshoot of the New York subway vigilantes, the Guardian Angels, have identified no fewer than 21,000 paedophile websites.[10] It's not hard for surfing children to land in the Internet's extensive red-light district. And Cyberangels – most of whom are middle-class female homemakers – regularly infiltrate and attempt to secure evidence against discussion groups promoting child abuse, violence, or suicide.

TAKING THE R OPTION WITH COMMUNICATIONS

At the end of the day, face-to-face meeting matters. Only when you meet another person face-to-face do you benefit from the full range and depth of human communication. According to Professor Ekman, the human face is capable of producing more than ten thousand distinct expressions. So vital is eye contact to conversation that we spend up to 75 per cent of conversational time looking at the person we're talking to. When we can't see the other person's lips, we need him or her to speak up by about 15 decibels.[11]

In short, you simply can't 'read' another person properly unless you're there in the same room. You can't interpret the body language. You can't pick up those vital downtime opportunities when the real business is done – over coffee, lingering in the corridor, waiting for a meeting to begin. Every day, countless London executives fly across the Atlantic and back to do just a few hours' face-to-face business in New York. Why not use a videoconference call? Because they know that meeting people in person produces greater buy-in, whether it's to a company strategy document or a sales contract.

In other words, there is an absolute, bottom-line benefit to being with someone that technology can't yet reproduce. At the same time, it's important in communications technology to distinguish trends that may undermine relationships from trends that the next generation will simply absorb and adapt to.

Significantly, a recent MORI poll on the use of text messaging by British 15–24 year-olds revealed that 37 per cent have used a text message to say 'I love you,' 81 per cent have used text messages to co-ordinate social arrangements, and one per cent have even used it to propose marriage.[12] Times change. As with the Amish, the R option is not about embracing or rejecting technology outright, but about being discerning and selective in its use.

1. Use the technology to help you prioritise

Being able to communicate at all hours in effect forces you to prioritise between relationships. You can't talk to everyone simultaneously – no matter how adept you are at multitasking. So which conversations require your immediate and undivided attention – and which can be deferred until later?

No one is forcing you to take a call at the moment it comes in. It may be worth examining how you use technologies that allow you to divert calls and take messages – and also how far you give out phone numbers and email addresses outside the circle of your closest and most important relationships.

For men, particularly, it can be ego massage to take calls when you're in the middle of talking to someone else. But what does your willingness to be interrupted say about your commitment to the person you're talking to?

2. Make the technology serve your goals

Technology isn't an end in itself. In relational terms, communications technologies like the mobile phone, networked computers, or email are useful if they enable you to manage your relationships more effectively. The implications of this may need some careful thought.

Giving your children mobile phones so you can stay in contact when you're not around can be a helpful security measure. But phoning doesn't compensate for your absence. How we envisage using the technology may then raise other issues to do with balancing priorities and ensuring enough face-to-face time with those who need us.

Most of the really important conversations you have with your partner or children will happen *without* phones or email. Communication devices can help families and friends do things together – but you have to be doing something together before the technology can help you.

3. Recognise the technology's limits

By nature, brief messages are easy to misinterpret. For this reason, it's worth being careful how you use technologies like email – especially as we now have to respond to so many messages and do it so fast.

Often you can save both time and misunderstanding by phoning instead of emailing, by replying only if necessary, and by placing relationship management higher on your list of priorities. You may want to look at how you handle apparently aggressive incoming mail. Do you shoot back from the hip and badmouth the sender to colleagues in the same room? Or do you give yourself some cool-down time and check what's behind the communication?

4. Ensure the technology doesn't weaken your close relationships

Businesses tend to introduce and upgrade communication technologies in an organised and comprehensive way. After all, you don't raise your productivity by networking only three of your fifty desktop PCs.

By contrast, social groups like families absorb new technologies in an ad hoc manner. Often, the younger members embrace the new devices and grow to rely on them, while older members hold back. In her study of Silicon Valley, Jan Lueck notes that 'an ageing mother found her role as family centre being eroded by her children's constant email contact. She was now superfluous as the siblings talked directly to each other and not through her.'[13]

The R option in this kind of area might include looking at how family members can keep in step technologically.

It's not impossible to provide technophobic grandparents with email – or to assign a younger relative to keep the system working and show Granny how to check for messages. The issue is whether technology is allowed to divide people and isolate them, or whether it provides excuses for greater integration and contact.

5. Use the technology to power your networks

Email, particularly, provides an invaluable tool for maintaining social networks. No doubt, people will send real snail-mail Christmas cards for years to come, but the network defined by the Christmas card list (and the sometimes arduous duty of writing all those cards) is fast being transformed.

Using email and family or personal websites serves the useful purpose of making information available widely and quickly, and will get easier as more people go online. Changes of address can be broadcast almost instantly, important pieces of news cut and pasted without the implied insult of sending photocopies by post.

The danger lies in confusing information with interaction. Having a website – in effect, the equivalent of pinning family news to your front door – is no substitute for personal contact with others.

In an age when blocks of information can be pasted seamlessly from one email to the next, it's easy to overload your contact with unwanted facts. Deciding how much to write to whom is becoming increasingly important. So, too, is the sending of photographs. And, so, too, is the plain old personal touch – an inquiry, shared memory or detail directed to that particular person, and no one else.

---

1   This and following quote from Howard Rheingold, 'Look Who's Talking,' *Wired*, January 1999.

2   In the UK, for example, a recent NOP survey showed that by the beginning of 2001, half of all children aged 7–16 possessed a mobile phone. By the same point, 85% of those aged 16–24 had accessed the Internet (up from 69% in July 2000). Home Internet usage in the UK quadrupled in the last four years of the twentieth century.

3   In case you were wondering, the message was: 'What hath God wrought.'

4   Jan English-Lueck, *Technology and Social Change: The Effects on Family and Community*, an address to the COSSA Congressional Seminar, 19 June, 1998. The full text can be found at:
    http://www.sjsu.edu/depts/anthropology/svcp/SVCPcosa.html.

5   Thomas L. Freedman, *New York Times*, reproduced in *The Week*, Feb 10, 2001.

6   Even letters of complaint are apt to begin with 'Dear Sir/Madam' – one of a range of mechanisms limiting the damage the content of a letter can do to the writer's relationship with the recipient. By contrast, email currently relies on slightly ambiguous mood symbols (J or :-) for 'happy,' >:-O for 'angry and shouting.'

7   See the survey commissioned by Novell: *Shaming, Blaming and Flaming:*

Corporate Miscommunication in the Digital Age, reported in the *Daily Telegraph,* 3 June 1997.

8 Reported by Andy Hobsbawm, 'Visual Anonymity,' *Financial Times,* 29 April 2000.

9 Robert Kraut, Michael Patterson, Vicki Lundmark, Sara Kriesler, Tridas Mukopadhyay & William Scherlis, of Carnegie Mellon University, 'Internet Paradox: A social technology that reduces social involvement and psychological wellbeing?'. *American Psychologist,* Vol.53, no.9, pp.1017–1031, September 1998. Quotations taken from p.1017 and p.1029.

10 Interestingly, according to the Cyberangels' CEO, Parry Aftab, 'Managing a virtual organisation is very difficult because I never get to look in anybody's eyes.' To compensate, she vets all volunteers personally online. See Jonathan Green, 'Closing the Net,' *Times Magazine,* 22 May 1999.

11 Source: Professor Paul Ekman in the BBC programme *About Face*, broadcast 2001.

12 MORI Polls & Surveys, *I Just Text To Say I Love You,* 5 September 2000. The article can be found at: http://www.mori.com/polls/2000/lycos.shtml.

13 Jan English-Lueck, *op.cit.*

CHAPTER FOUR

MANAGEMENT

The time gap and the leverage in the futures market means that the futures are far more volatile than the share index itself....

For a few seconds a difference would open up between the Osaka and Singapore prices and that's when we went into action.

'OK', I told Fernando. 'Bought 200 at 580.'

'Cheers, Nick, I've sold at 590.'

We had sold in Osaka and bought the same contracts in Singapore for a £16,000 profit. And the risk? Two and a half seconds before, the market would have seen us coming like a big red London bus and moved up...[1]

This is how the 'rogue trader' Nick Leeson describes a day's work on the Singapore Stock Exchange. His colleagues called it 'switching' – simultaneously buying and selling a security to exploit differences in the price quoted on different exchanges. It's perfectly legal, and Barings Bank paid Leeson a six-figure salary to do it.

But during his three-year posting to Singapore, Leeson was making far bigger and riskier trades that Barings in London knew nothing about. By early 1995, the financial obligations he'd racked up in Error Account 88888 had reached a staggering $60 *billion* – roughly a hundred times the entire reported capital reserves of the bank.

In the catastrophe that followed, one question required an urgent answer. How could one trader have accumulated debts gargantuan enough to put Barings into receivership – *without anybody noticing?*

WHY BARINGS WENT DOWN

The Bank of England's report agreed with Barings chairman Peter Baring that 'the failure of controls was absolute'.[2] Elsewhere the investigators blamed 'inadequate communication', 'lack of proper supervision', and the absence of 'clearly laid down reporting lines for Leeson'.

But you can have all the controls and reporting lines you want in an organisation: they will achieve little if the people concerned don't use them. And it's clear that – for a variety of reasons – this wasn't happening at Barings.

Leeson himself is blunt about it:

The only good thing about hiding losses from these people [Barings senior management] was that it was so easy. They were always too busy and too self-important, and were always on the telephone. They had the attention span of a gnat. They could not make the time to work through a sheet of numbers and spot that it didn't add up...they never dared ask me any basic questions, since they were afraid of looking stupid about not understanding futures and options.[3]

It's asking a lot of Leeson to be impartial. Nevertheless, an underlying problem at Barings emerges fairly clearly. Both on the formal level (of procedures and controls) and on the informal level (of constructive interaction), the bank was sunk by dysfunctional relationships.

A number of factors conspired to make things difficult. There was clearly a culture gap between the top brass in London and the brash young traders doing the deals. There was probably also, as Leeson suggests, a skills gap arising from the rapid pace of technological change. Not least, we should remember that winning strategies on the money markets are a kind of intellectual property you fight to protect even from your own boss.

On the one hand, then, Barings staff worked in an intensely competitive environment where secrecy even from your own colleagues was part of the culture. And on the other hand, relationships between London and Singapore had become so stretched that supervision was almost impossible. As Leeson pleads: 'Nobody stopped me.'[4]

THE SOFT ISSUES ARE THE HARD ISSUES

In a business context, relationships have suddenly come to the surface as a key factor in producing success. 'A new consensus has emerged', says Tim Morgan, former CEO of the Industrial Society. 'This sees organisations as living systems in which relationships are much more important than structures and processes.'

For a long time relationships were considered a 'soft issue' in business. This was partly because the idea of business relationships being good or bad seemed to belong in ethics, and thus to fall beyond the ambit of serious business theory. Partly, also, it was because – unlike profit and loss – relationships are hard to reduce to numbers.

Nevertheless, the top companies on both sides of the Atlantic increasingly see the value of trying. Forty per cent of Most Admired Companies now chart retention, career development, and other employee-oriented measurements – triple the percentage of companies that don't make the list.[5]

One of them – the British oil giant BP Amoco – maps the progress of its 'people' targets – qualitative performance measures like innovation, mutual trust, respect, teamwork, and diversity – on a quarterly basis. 'Like many of the companies on this year's Global Most Admired list, BP Amoco recognises that achievements in these areas are just as important to the success of the company as revenues, profits, and other financial measures.'[6]

Significantly, a study in the USA recently showed that about 40 per cent of new management recruits fail within the first 18 months, concluding: 'Failure to build good relationships with peers and subordinates is the culprit an overwhelming 82 per cent of the time.'[7]

Relationships are crucial to business at four levels:[8]

At a strategic level

All business organisations are searching for competitive advantage. To achieve this, they can look to their particular product design – but competitors can usually replicate that fairly quickly. They can rely on their level of service – but, of course, this does not differentiate the product. They can develop a brand image, which is worth a lot – but the expense is usually considerable and success cannot be guaranteed.

Consequently, the most important way a business can develop a strategic competitive advantage is through the *network of relationships* it develops with customers, suppliers and other stakeholders – especially employees. In the words of management guru Robert Waterman, 'The key to strategic success is mainly this: building relationships with customers, suppliers, and employees that are exceptionally hard for competitors to duplicate.'[9]

Unlike products, relationships are tough to replicate quickly. You can't buy them in. And as a result, what might be called the 'relational architecture' a business has built up over the years can be a massive source of competitive advantage.

At a cultural level

The term 'culture' gets used fairly sloppily in business. In fact, culture exists within – and is a quality of – the relationships that hold a business together. The culture can work either for you or against you. When we say that the culture 'is receptive to change,' we generally mean that relationships are strong enough to accommodate new patterns of working without a breakdown of trust. Cultures resistant to change almost always reveal weak relationships and low levels of mutual confidence – most notably between levels of management.

Relationships, then, give us a more precise and useful language to deal with so-called 'cultural' issues. An example of this is provided by Amerco, where in a workshop for Human Resource managers, participants explored ways to make friendship work for the benefit of the company – for example, by calling a friend for a chat and asking for help with a work issue.[10]

At an operational level

No company can survive without policies, procedures and systems. But again, what we are really talking about here is relationships. A system is a relational pattern – a statement of who should relate to whom about what. But that pattern has to be made to work in real relationships between real people. If those people don't get on, no system is going to save you.

Conversely, it's often the case that inadequate, outdated, or clumsily-applied systems can be made to work if actual working relationships provide the 'lubricating oil'. An American retailer called the Container Store, for example, has established some simple operational principles. Among these are: 'We treat our employees as humans', and 'Treat people as you want to be treated.' The company also gives its employees full access to the company ledger. The outcome: a company whose staff turnover is a fraction of the industry's, losing just 28 per cent of its full-time salespeople a year, compared with the industry average of 74 per cent.[11]

At a personal level

For you, the individual employee, it is the relationships at the office that make your work pleasant or intolerable. Overbearing bosses, office politics, bullying, sexual harassment, unhealthy competitiveness between individuals – all these are signs of dysfunction in relationships. And a mismanaged relational environment impacts directly on morale, motivation, and productivity. Hence the intense interest shown by top companies in setting up relationships in such a way as to retain their employees.

According to a recent investigation by *Fortune*, the hundred 'best companies to work for in America' all provide 'a supportive and challenging workplace in which communication is encouraged, ingenuity rewarded, and internal mobility expected' – a situation which is 'maintained by managers who are both visible and accessible'.[12]

HOW DO YOU MEASURE RELATIONSHIPS IN A MANAGEMENT CONTEXT?

If your company isn't doing much to improve office relationships, the reason may lie in the difficulty of measuring how good, or bad, those relationships are.

In 1995, a report from a leading British think-tank concluded, 'Many companies acknowledge that measures of the strength of the relationship are predictive of future financial performance.' It added, however: 'More work is needed to find robust measures for the full range of key relationships.'[13]

The mistake often made is to assume that relationships automatically exist in business – either because the management structure says they do, or just because people are working in the same building.

But relationships *don't* automatically exist. The structure that makes you my line manager doesn't in itself provide the trust and mutual understanding we need to make the connection work. In a busy office, or, worse, if one of us is teleworking, forming any kind of meaningful relationship may be very hard.

This distinction between relationships 'on paper' and relationships 'in practice' is crucial. It's the second, not the first, that fuels successful enterprise. But how do you make paper relationships work on the ground? Isn't it just a matter of whether two people happen to get along?

Well, no it isn't. If you want to get along with a colleague, or if you're a manager and you want two employees to get along, then first of all you need to make *room to relate*.[14]

FIVE WAYS OF MAKING ROOM TO RELATE

Organisations are notoriously bad at doing this. Most offices are driven by an endless stream of tasks and deadlines, and it's simply assumed that employees will have enough social skills to co-operate in getting the tasks done and the deadlines met. It's rare for an employer to step back and ask, 'How can we ensure that working relationships here boost our productivity?'

But if you make room to relate – either as a managerial policy or as a personal decision – you are, in effect, enabling office relationships to work for you and not against you. And relationships are a powerful ally.

At the heart of the issue is removing, as far as possible, the various kinds of clutter that get in between people and stop them getting to know one another better. The clutter comes in various sorts – including unsynchronised timetables and differences of status as well as sheer physical distance.

You 'make room' in five ways:[15]

1. Directness

First, by making room for *direct* communication. Email, mobiles and videoconferencing are all fabulous assets. But relationships just don't work without a certain amount of direct, face-to-face communication. Important relationships, and important situations, demand directness – hence the finding by the Leadership Trust that more than half of managers find it more difficult to motivate and lead remote workers than other employees.[16]

A staff grievance can't be solved by emailing from the other side of the world. As soon as possible, you need to sit across a table and look that person in the eye. Personal meetings increase your ability to pick up danger signals – you learn far more by reading faces than you do by reading voices or text. They also make other people feel you're accessible – especially if you don't use your PA to keep people out.

Direct communication stimulates openness and disclosure, and gives people time to raise the kinds of questions and problems it's hard to air on the phone. That means fewer misunderstandings further down the road, and less chance of junior staff getting thrown in the deep end unprepared.

2. Continuity

A second way to make room for relationships is by giving them *continuity* over time. Recently, the Relationships Foundation carried out an audit for a leading law firm. We found that pressure of work was causing non-partners to leave the firm early in their careers, driving a high staff turnover. The low retention rate was a destabilising factor, affecting morale and leading to the loss of important clients. It also resulted in high additional costs in recruitment and induction to replace staff who left.[17] Two-thirds of the partners and non-partners we interviewed said there wasn't enough time to build relationships.

A certain amount of personnel change is invigorating for an organisation. But you only reap the benefits of trust and mutual understanding if relationships are allowed to settle and grow. In the USA, the average 32-year-old has worked for nine companies.[18] It's not surprising, perhaps, that only 53 per cent of American employees can say they trust the people they work with 'a lot'.[19]

If you're a manager, keeping regular contact with line staff helps you provide adequate monitoring and quality control. It keeps teamwork co-ordinated and focused. And it helps you manage change by encouraging good handovers at points of staff transition. Continuity matters too in relationships outside the organisation. If you don't see customers often enough, you know less about them. As a result, you can't meet their needs with the required precision, and they don't feel cared for.

3. Multiplexity

A third way to make room for relationships is by meeting people in more places than just the office: playing a round of golf, meeting families at a social evening, going on staff retreats.

This kind of *multiplexity* is surprisingly effective, because it breaks the mould of your expectations. People behave differently outside the workplace. You see what other relationships they have, what drives them, how they deal with non-work situations.

This added depth in itself tends to enhance trust and a sense of mutual accountability. It also gives you an insight into the pressures a colleague's under from directions other than work. You're better able to anticipate crises, and able to give more effective support. Not least, seeing people 'out of context' may reveal skills and potentials you never knew they had.

4. Parity

A fourth way to make room for relationships is to narrow the power differentials. This kind of *parity* is more of an issue *between* management levels than across them, and most scope for personal action lies in your relationships with those who report to you.[20]

One key question is how much participation in decision-making you encourage from those who work for you. Low involvement can result in reduced morale, weakened commitment and stifled innovation – with a consequent impact on quality of output and initiative in problem solving.

Another issue is fairness. If one person on your team thinks another person is getting preferential treatment, the result will be dissent, undermined morale, and loss of motivation.

As the British union leader Jack Jones put it on one occasion, 'There's never been a strike about pay, only about pay differentials.' Similarly, if you don't distribute rewards fairly, you can easily weaken co-operation and incentivise risk rather than team-building. Not least, fairness reduces the likelihood of industrial action and tribunal claims.

5. Commonality

A last way to make room for relationships in organisations is by encouraging overlap in people's values and goals. This idea of *commonality* is fairly well understood at corporate level, though not always effectively applied. When the US software manufacturer Lotus added 'Have fun!' to its list of basic company values, Americans understood instinctively. However, workers at its Dutch operation found the invitation intrusive.[21]

Cultural differences can always divide us – even if we were raised in the same town. But building a sense of shared identity, and constructing a set of genuinely shared objectives, both enhances communication between company employees and drives higher productivity.[22]

TAKING THE R OPTION IN MANAGEMENT

Making room to relate comes down to five issues: directness, continuity, multiplexity, parity, and commonality.

One useful feature of these 'preconditions for good relating' is that they can be measured. As the Relationships Foundation has demonstrated, it is possible to audit key relationships within and around an organisation (for instance, between customers and suppliers), identifying the risks associated with weak relationships and their likely impact on organisational performance. It is then possible to indicate how changes should be made in order to render relationships more effective and thus improve business performance.

Making room for relationships is also a powerful way of changing your own business conduct and performance, irrespective of company policy. So here are some ideas for you personally.

1. Map your work relationships

A simple exercise for exploring the R option in your organisation begins with drawing up a simple relational 'radar diagram'. The diagram shown in Figure 1 was originally devised to help individuals map out their own relational base, using a set of concentric circles. A person's personal relationships are entered by name (represented by crosses on the diagram), and their level of significance measured by the distance from the central point.

The diagram can easily be adapted to an organisational context by replacing the main headings with your key relationships at work, both internally (e.g. team members, superiors, subordinates) and externally (e.g. clients/customers, suppliers, contractors, peers in other organisations).

There's nothing sophisticated about this diagram. It's just a visual device for identifying those working relationships that – for whatever reason – you feel need most attention.

You may find that most or all of these fall inside the organisation (if you're concerned with management issues), or outside (if you operate as a consultant). Either way, are there any key relationships to which you are not giving enough attention? If so, how can you give more? And how successful are you in prioritising those relationships that are most important to you?

2. Assess your own relational performance

You can use the five ideas of *directness, continuity, multiplexity, parity,* and *commonality* to assess how much room you're making for your relationships in the workplace. Most people try to build work relationships. But you may not be building the ones that matter. And it's often easier to bury yourself at your desk than make the effort to relate. Think through the following questions.

Directness

- How much time do you spend in face-to-face contact with people you are close to in the workplace?

- To what extent are you accessible to people with whom you have an important relationship?

- Are you responsive in getting back to people when they make demands on you?

- In your dealings with people, are you essentially a talker or a listener – and what is the impact of this?

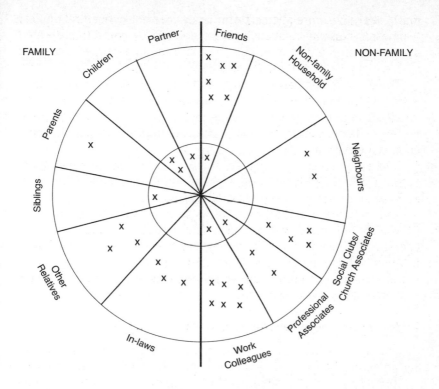

Figure 1 **An individual's relational base**

Continuity

- Do you take time at the start of a relationship to develop a thorough understanding of the other person's perspective?

- Do you have sufficient contact with key people in the workplace?

- What is happening to the level of trust and understanding in the main relationships you have at work?

Multiplexity

- How much do you know about the broader responsibilities and lives of the people you work with?

- Do you have a good understanding of your colleagues' roles/skills and experience?

- In addition to formal contact, do you initiate informal contacts with colleagues?

Parity

- Do you seek the active participation of your colleagues in decisions which affect them?

- Do you credit people with their contribution to the work?

- Are risk and reward shared fairly with colleagues?

- In whose workspace do you hold a discussion?

Commonality

- Do you and your colleagues (suppliers, customers, investors) have a common view of the goals of the business and the means of achieving them?

- Do you understand the culture within which your colleagues operate?

- Are you aware of the possibility of misinterpreting actions and making false assumptions?

- Do you use the diversity of your team to create richness and creativity in your work?

- When there are disagreements between you and your colleagues, do you handle them well?

3. Develop your relational skills

Over the last year, I (Michael) have had contact with two multinationals. The first is a partnership, the second a plc. In both organisations, there was a major issue with the most senior staff. They didn't know how to relate to the people they were managing.

They might be brilliant lawyers, outstandingly good at making financial decisions, good team players at board level. But when it came to communicating effectively with their teams, motivating staff, and handling workplace conflicts, they were just beginners.

Most of us need to develop our relational skills throughout our business careers. This is partly about learning to think relationally in all areas of life – which is the subject of this book. Partly it's about attending good courses in the practicalities of good relating. Relevant areas for training currently available include: listening skills, counselling skills, communication skills, handling customer or supplier relationships, and handling of personnel.

4. Review the company's structure and operations in relational terms

If you have the opportunity to exert an influence on your company's structure and operations, the first step is to evaluate systematically how the company works in relationship terms.

Here are some of the areas you may want to consider:

- Use of flexitime to ease home/work tensions.

- Office layout, including allocation of personnel between different sites, use of open plan or closed offices, positioning of desks with respect to ease of communication.

- Commitment to meetings between managers and their teams – in terms of frequency, regularity and time given to discussion.

- Clarity of, and staff buy-in to, company goals.

- Systems and thoroughness of annual staff appraisal.

- Company provision for those with illness or other emergency difficulties.

- Extent of income disparities between the top and bottom of the organisation.

- Opportunities to meet partners and relatives of work colleagues – for instance, at office parties and outings.

- Opportunities for job sharing.

5. Treat relationships as ends, not just means

It's possible to value relationships in business simply because they assist in the immediate goal of making higher profits. You encourage employees to smile at customers in order to make the sale.

Now this is fine as far as it goes – and no doubt at the supermarket checkout most of us would rather be smiled at than greeted with a surly scowl. But a purely economic motive for developing a good 'client manner' seldom survives a period of real pressure. And even when things are going well, hard-pressed consumers have a remarkable ability to discern genuine goodwill from a forced grin.

By contrast, in a company with an ethos that sees good relationships as an end as well as a means – in other words, an ethos of service delivery to customers and building relationships with suppliers and other stakeholders – it's much easier for front-line staff to be sincere. In the long term, it's this sincerity that builds genuine loyalty between the business and those who have dealings with it. And there is the satisfaction for employees of knowing they have acted with integrity towards customers and suppliers.

---

1   Nick Leeson, *Rogue Trader* (London: Little, Brown, 1996), pp.33, 34, 35.
2   *Report Of The Board Of Banking Supervision Inquiry Into The Circumstances Of The Collapse Of Barings* (London: HMSO Publications Centre, 1995), paragraph 13:10.
3   Nick Leeson, *op.cit.,* pp.160–161,177.
4   *Ibid.*
5   Nicholas Stein, 'Global Most Admired: Measuring People Power' in *Fortune*, 2 October 2000.
6   *Ibid.*
7   *Fortune*, 22 June 1998.
8   We are indebted to Mr Paul Sandham for applying relational thinking to this area.
9   Robert Waterman, *The Frontiers of Excellence: Learning from Companies that put People First* (London: Nicholas Brealey, 1994), p.170.
10 See Arlie Russell Hochschild, *The Time Bind* (Second Owl Books, 2001), p.19.
11 Daniel Roth, 'My Job At The Container Store' in *Fortune,* 10 January 2000.
12 Nicholas Stein, 'Winning the War to Keep Top Talent' in *Fortune,* 29 May 2000.
13 RSA Inquiry, Tomorrow's Company, *The role of business in a changing world* (London: RSA, 1995) p.11.
14 For a fuller treatment of this, see Michael Schluter and David Lee, *The R Factor* (London: Hodder & Stoughton, 1993). *The R Factor* can be ordered from the Relationships Foundation or through its website
        (www.relationshipsfoundation.org/books/Index.html) for £7.99 plus P & P.
15 The approach outlined in this chapter is the basis of Relational Auditing, a method developed by the Relationships Foundation and used successfully as an auditing tool in both private and public sector organisations in the UK. For more information, see www.relationshipsfoundation.org/assessing_relationships/Index.html

16 *Financial Times,* 8 May 2000, p.34, 'Chats over coffee hard to replace' by Alison Maitland.

17 Damage caused by losing employees can be severe. According to John Challenger, CEO of outplacement firm Challenger Gray & Christmas, 'Companies now face the most competitive job market in decades, and losing workers can savage a bottom line. When you consider lost productivity and replacement costs, a single defection can cost a company between $50,000 and $100,000. It gets even worse if you lose top talent, with their vast stores of intellectual capital gleaned over years at the company. Knowing how to retain top people in this challenging environment can be a real competitive advantage.' Quoted by Nicholas Stein, 'Winning the War to Keep Top Talent' in *Fortune,* 29 May 2000.

18 *Financial Times,* 26 July 2000. Note that, according to the US Census Bureau, over half (56.4%) of all US employees have been in their current jobs less than four years. For workers age 25–34, the figure rises to 69.2%. (See: *Statistical Abstract of the United States, 2000, No. 664*: 'Distribution of workers by tenure with current employer, 1998').

19 See http://www.cfsv.org/communitysurvey. If anything, the situation seems to be worse in the UK, where the Industrial Society has discovered that 93% of managers do not trust their employees (*Financial Times,* 26 July 2000. Article by Will Hutton and John Knell, 'A new network economy is breeding a less loyal and more independent worker'. Inside Track – Born Free – Viewpoint).

20 This is less true in company structures outside the plc. In the John Lewis Partnership, for example, even the checkout staff are partners in the ownership of the company and have a say in its management.

21 Lisa Hoecklin, *Managing Cultural Differences: Strategies for Competitive Advantage* (Wokingham, England: Addison-Wesley, 1995), p.117.

22 Mark Scholefield. *The Impact of Culture on Relationships and Ways of Coping with Cultural Difference* (Relationships Foundation Review Paper, March 2001). This paper is available on the Relationships Foundation's website at www.relationshipsfoundation.org/cgi-bin/download.pl?type=research_paper.

CHAPTER FIVE

MONEY

I (David) once met a woman who'd fallen out with a relative over an inheritance. Her mother had left some property, and the argument had never been resolved. It was so bad, she said, they hadn't spoken to each other since. I asked how long ago this happened. She replied: 'Almost twenty years.'

Money divides. But money also binds people together.

Back in the 1960s, the family business my (Michael's) father was running in London came close to going under when an employee over-traded in one of the commodity markets. What saved the company was the willingness of a close friend of my father to buy shares when the share value was practically zero.

The investment kept the company in business and quickly put it on the road to a recovery which has enabled it to hold its own until the present day. It also cemented an already strong relationship between the investor and our family.

MONEY AND THE PROBLEM OF UNFAIRNESS

'Money couldn't buy friends', Spike Milligan once observed, 'but you got a better class of enemy.'[1]

Creating enmity, in fact, is one of money's most frequent side effects. Because human beings need and want the things money buys, marked differences in access to money are apt to arouse feelings of envy, injustice, or contempt. It doesn't seem 'fair' that some people should have a lot more than others.

This effect operates even in close relationships – as the example of the inheritance suggests. More marriage break-ups are caused by arguments over money than by any other single factor.[2]

But the effect also works at a much more general level. Sharing an economic system actually facilitates relationships, in the sense that many relationships are created around the earning and spending of money. But differences in wealth also create social divisions.

For example, once you factor in annual bonuses and share options, the salary package differential between the Tesco Chief Executive and a Tesco checkout clerk is close to 100:1.[3] And this sets up a whole set of secondary barriers. They'll live in different areas. They'll send their children to different schools. They'll take holidays in different places.

Large salaries, of course, may be acceptable from the company's point of view, on the grounds that a talented CEO is worth paying for. It may well be worthwhile for Barclays to give their chief executive a salary of ten million pounds, because a really effective chief executive may well increase corporate earnings in a large company like Barclays by as much as £500 million.

The larger the differential, however, the more likely it is that top managers will be seen as 'fat cats' who are motivated more by the prospect of personal gain than by any serious, long-term commitment to the company and its stakeholders. In that situation, personal empathy diminishes between those at the top and bottom of the pay scale, and the widening wealth differential too easily implies a distinction in worth or dignity. No wonder top managers can find it so hard to get alongside their workers.

Across a whole society, this problem reproduces itself on a larger scale. Particularly when poverty at the lower end threatens basic provision of food, shelter and warmth, the sense of unfairness may find expression in civil unrest.[4] Similarly, at the international level, wealth differentials underlie disagreement over key environmental objectives, with poorer nations – not unreasonably – asking why they should have to foot the bill to meet targets set by their richer neighbours.

HOW SPENDING AFFECTS YOUR CLOSE RELATIONSHIPS

But relationships aren't only affected by the amount of money you have. They're also affected by how you spend it. The more responsibilities you have – to partner, parents, or children – the more your *use* of money becomes a live issue.

Consumer debt has been an acute problem in Britain and the USA for over twenty years.[5] Saddled with repayments they cannot afford, earners find their relationships with family members under increasing stress. As one respondent to a survey put it:

You can't help falling out, not because you start disliking each other, but because things are on top of you. And then again your standards go down. You get angry with the kids. Then you can't afford to buy them all the things they need.[6]

There is a positive side too, of course. Financial hardship can, if rightly handled, encourage people to 'pull together' and strengthen relationships. Also, money can be used deliberately to enhance intimacy – spending on loved ones at Christmas, surprising someone with a bunch of flowers, or treating children to ice cream.

IS USE OF MONEY AN 'I' OR A 'WE' DECISION?

Today we talk about *my* bank account, *my* insurance policy, *my* pension, *my* tax return. Indeed, the policy of taxing people as individuals, and thus of giving tax concessions to individuals (as with, for example, the UK's Individual Savings Account), encourages the individual to function as an autonomous economic unit.

We should recognise the advantages of this. For one thing, it obliges us to take more responsibility for our own financial affairs. And for another, it means that women have the freedom to earn, save, and buy on a par with men.

But there are disadvantages, too. Inevitably, looking out for yourself financially makes you that bit more cautious about merging your assets with a partner and operating as a 'joint business' – even if there are strong arguments relationally for doing so. Also, at a wider level, a society which encourages its members to look to their own interests financially will find it harder to increase funding for schools by raising direct or indirect taxation.

Western societies tend to forget that money functions as a kind of social glue, flowing most easily down established lines of affection and trust. One striking international example of this is the Kenyan *harambee*. The term, literally meaning 'pull together,' was coined by President Kenyatta as a way of mobilising funds for local projects. It's a kind of charity event. Someone throws a party for friends and neighbours, and passes the hat around. Such relationship-based fundraising has founded many schools, and sent many sick children for essential surgery abroad.

Anyone who's participated in an investment syndicate will know that sharing on-going financial risk and reward brings together people from very different walks of life. Other examples include businesses bought out by employees, who then become jointly responsible for the enterprise and thus more motivated to work for its success.

This kind of co-operation and resource-pooling lies at the root of mutual insurance, which originated in the need of small nineteenth-century fishing communities to spread the risks of a notoriously dangerous occupation.

It has also undergirded the UK's fast-vanishing building society movement. In an individualistic culture, nothing is more alluring than the prospect of a plump and immediate windfall payout in exchange for your support in demutualising a building society and turning it into a limited company.

But in their eagerness to strip the society's assets, few investors or carpetbaggers pause to consider what the relative merits of mutual and plc structures might be – or whether future savers and borrowers might thank them for leaving the reserves where they are. Are they in fact cashing-in the savings made largely by previous generations?

WE IMPACT THE WORLD AROUND US
IN THE WAY WE USE OUR MONEY

I (David) once answered an advertisement for a second-hand CD-ROM of the *Encyclopaedia Britannica*. The price was good, and the small classified ad explained that the CD was an 'unwanted gift'. When I got there, however, all was not what it seemed.

The seller turned out to have an almost limitless supply of 'unwanted gifts', all of them unpackaged CDs with the content scribbled across them in black felt-tip pen.

Now admittedly, bootleg CDs aren't like hard drugs. From the consumer's point of view, they meet the main specifications of quality and price. Software reproduces efficiently, and discs are cheap. I could easily have persuaded myself that I was getting what I wanted without being made to pay through the nose. What was the harm?

Well, the harm is essentially relational. Leaving aside the small question of legality, situations like this force you to ask who's receiving the benefit of your trade.

I'm prepared to allow that this gentleman might have had a large and needy family on the brink of starvation (though the size of his Chelsea flat rather weighed against this). But without a doubt, buying bootleg CDs deprives the producer company and its employees – not to mention its employees' dependants – of money that is rightfully theirs.

This is not abstract morality. My purchasing decision is a trip switch directing the flow of money through the dense wiring of the market economy. What I do has consequences for other people.

Similar kinds of connection occur through investments. For example, if I put my money into NatWest – or any other bank, for that matter – I will receive interest each quarter on my savings. But I'll have no idea how or where that interest is generated. It could be that NatWest lent the money to a company making wheelchairs for the disabled. Or the interest may have come from a company selling into the international arms trade.

In reality, no doubt, the bank obtains its return on loans to a wide variety of organisations. But the point is that I don't know – and probably won't much care – what those organisations are. Across the world, countless companies are using my money and paying me for the privilege – but because the bank acts as intermediary, it's impossible for me as the saver to have any direct link with the companies using my cash.

Another side of the same issue springs on to your computer screen if you manage online investments. Stock markets increasingly act like race meetings. Assuming I'm a shrewd player, I'll probably look at the 'form' of the companies I invest in. I'll want to know something about the fundamentals of the industry, and the general background against which share prices in that sector are moving.

But if I buy a block of shares in Unilever, it's unlikely that I'll now think of myself as that company's part-owner. Nor will I consider how my actions may affect the lives of some proportion of Unilever's thousands of employees, the communities where those employees live, or the environments impacted by Unilever's operations.

Such information has no bearing on my goal to select, and back, the companies most likely to be stock market winners. Indeed, as Internet-based, short-term share dealing expands, investment will only become more speculative and narrowly focused on current prices and immediate trends. This week I own part of Unilever; next week I may have sold up and moved on.

TAKING THE R OPTION WITH MONEY

The R option with money begins with a recognition that money plays a big part in relationships. All our close relationships involve the handling of money. And in today's global economy, world markets give us slender but tangible links to vast numbers of people we will never see.

Clearly, how you apply the R option will depend a lot on your particular circumstances. But there's a range of possibilities.

1. Spend money to develop friendships

Though money affects relationships whether we like it or not, most of us still have a nagging conviction that money and relationships don't mix. The phrase 'I only did it for the money' catches well our shared distrust of money as a motive. Outside the realm of paid employment – and perhaps even within it – we feel that people should be driven by something more dignified than financial gain.

Clearly it's important not to be too sanctimonious about this. But at least in the matter of spending, it's possible to ask: Is this purchase going to benefit only me, or will it help to build my relationships?

For example, if I have £75 or $100 to blow at the end of the month, do I treat myself to something I've been wanting to buy, or use the money to fund a good night out with my friends or partner? In the first case, the beneficiary is me. In the second, the benefit is mutual. I'm not arguing that one option is always right and the other always wrong – only that the distinction should be remembered.

There are dangers, of course, in appearing to solicit favours, or in splashing money around because you're chronically insecure. Nevertheless, it remains true that generous people are liked. I (David) was really touched ten years ago when a friend from Hong Kong bought a small tricycle for my daughter. There were no strings attached. He was just demonstrating – in hard cash – his commitment to our friendship.

2. Direct your spending to achieve social results

There's a similar principle at work in the way we act as consumers.

Consumer power is now a familiar concept as applied to the environment. You can buy conscientiously by choosing eco-friendly packaging, paper products with a high recycled content, free-range eggs, and organic vegetables.

In the same way, the R option ought to produce an 'R consumerism' – choosing products for their effect on the *social* environment. The seeds of this have been around for some time in the form of 'fair trade' tea and coffee, which guarantee higher returns to producers. Roughly one-in-six shoppers claims to frequently buy or boycott products because of the manufacturer's reputation.[7]

Ten years down the road, it's possible to envisage (for example) a charter mark for manufacturers who give a certain percentage of profits to specified social causes, or who can demonstrate exceptional performance in their relationships with employees, customers and suppliers.

Meanwhile an immediate issue for 'R' consumerism concerns not products but patterns of retailing. The nationwide shift towards mass, car-based shopping from superstores has fuelled a sharp decline among smaller shops. Over thirty years at the end of the twentieth century, the number of independent grocery outlets in the UK fell precipitously from 116,000 to 32,800.[8]

For the growing number of disadvantaged consumers – including lone parents, the physically disabled, and the low-income elderly – this closure of local shops puts quality of life at risk. Suddenly a simple trip to the shop becomes a major excursion, involving an unwelcome walk or a wait for a bus.

But these changes are not inevitable. Local retailers will stay in business if people use them. The continued presence of newsagents, chemists and general stores in your neighbourhood depends, in part, on your spending decisions.

3. Keep money management in the open with your partner

If you share your finances with another person, it's usually a good idea for that sharing within the relationship to be explicit. One partner may have more skill or experience in money management; but both partners have responsibility for the way money is used, and they need to communicate about it.

There are different ways of handling finances between two people. You can keep your earnings separate, but agree who pays which bills. Or you can both pay everything into a joint account. Either way, having the same goals and attitudes to money probably matters more than the mechanics.

Some specific guidelines on managing money within a relationship include the following:[9]

- Regardless of your respective earnings, divide responsibility fairly for routine financial decisions (bills, groceries) and major undertakings (house, car, vacations).

- Agree your financial goals together (long term as well as short term), and stick to them unless you both agree to change them.

- Make sure each of you has some money to spend as he/she likes. It doesn't help the relationship if one person has to ask the other for money.

- If you spend more than you earn, agree a budget together and don't deviate from it unless you both agree. If you can't work out your own budget, seek help.

4. Be aware of the relational consequences of investments

Nearly everyone makes some kind of investment – even if it's only running an interest-paying bank account. In conventional wisdom, the difference between a good investment and a bad one comes down to percentages. The best deposit account, the best stock, the best unit trust, is simply the one that delivers the best rate of return.

But taking the R option with investments involves more than finance. Every investment establishes a set of relationships. When you invest money, therefore, you are entitled to ask what those relationships are, and what effect your investment has on the other people it links you to. In this respect, different forms of investment perform in very different ways.

For example, as a shareholder, you are in effect part-owner of the company you invest in. Whether you like it or not, ownership brings responsibility. The problem is, it doesn't *feel* like that. Your insurance premiums and pension contributions go first to a financial institution, then to a fund manager, and only then into companies. As a result, the link between you as an investor and the company into which your money is being placed becomes, at best, obscure.

At present, the only solution to this is to put your money into so-called ethical funds – that is, funds that select companies on the basis of specified ethical criteria. The market is effective in defining good practice in the areas of general ethics and the physical environment. It's possible to invest through ethical or green pensions and unit trusts that screen companies for performance in these areas. There is a huge growth in the range of these funds and the different types of criteria they use. Their total worth worldwide is now in the region of $1.5 trillion.[10]

It's sometimes argued that ethical funds create a moral dilemma because you put your dependants at risk if you choose to invest for anything other than maximum return. The point is undermined somewhat by the fact that performance in ethical funds has tended to equal or slightly exceed that of competitors.[11] But even if this were not the case, it would probably be possible to invest a proportion of your money with ethical ends in view, without putting your dependants at serious risk. With thought and experience, external and domestic considerations with investment can be kept in balance.

5. Evaluate companies relationally

Clearly, the R option in share ownership could involve selecting only those companies with a proven track record of being 'relationship-friendly'. The problem revolves mainly around getting sufficient and relevant information. Among the key issues will be:

- Working conditions and the company's relationships with its staff.

- How responsive the company is to the needs of the communities in which it operates.

- What kind of social norms the company promotes through its advertising.

- The way the company treats its suppliers.

- To what extent staff are compelled to work unsocial hours in a way that interferes with friendships, family, and community.

- How great the pay differentials are between top management and shop floor.

- The quality of redundancy packages – and whether staff made redundant are helped to find new positions.

Although ethical trusts are increasingly making use of social audits to measure the company's impact on social relationships, we have not yet seen the development of R pensions and unit trusts that focus on the quality of relationships both inside and outside the company.

It is worth lobbying to have such funds set up. When they come on-stream, you will have a greater ability to focus your investments according to relational criteria, and consequently there will be a powerful incentive for plc managements to take relationships more seriously.

---

1   From Spike Milligan, *Puckoon* (1963).
2   In the USA, statistics show that as many as 70% of divorcing couples attribute the breakdown of their marriage to arguments about finances. See *State of California Employee Assistance Programme Newsletter,* Volume 5, No.8, February 1999.
3   The annual report 2000 for British supermarket giant Tesco shows Mr T.P. Leahy's total package as £1,173,000. According to a report from the Incomes Data Services, Sept 1999, quoted by Unison, a sales assistant earns an average of £5.16 an hour. Based on a 35-hour week, 52-week year, this comes to £9,391 a year – 0.8% of the CEO's package – although other elements may make up the sales assistant's total package.
4   The gap appears to have widened in both the UK and the USA. Between 1976 and 1998, the proportion of national wealth owned by the wealthiest 1% of the

population increased from 21% to 23%. Over the same period, the wealthiest 1% in the USA increased their holding of the nation's household wealth from 19% to 40%. Figures quoted by James Lardner, 'The Rich Get Richer,' cover story on *usnews.com*, 21 February 2000.

5   According to the US Census Bureau (*Statistical Abstract of the United States 2000*), 67.5% of American families have a credit card. Of these, 46.3% – almost half – only 'sometimes' or 'hardly ever' pay off the balance at the end of the month. According to NOP, 'In 2001, 45% of the UK adult population have a credit card. Before the wave of competition that hit the industry in 1994, the penetration rate was only 32%.' (NOP Financial Research Survey, May 2001 and NOP Financial Research Survey 1994/95).

     'Taking an average of the first six months of 2001, roughly 50% of Barclaycard's credit card customers paid interest (or borrowed) and did not pay their balance in full. This figure has remained stable in recent years.' Source: Barclaycard internal statistics.

6   Andrew Hartropp (ed.), *Families in Debt*, Jubilee Centre Research Paper No.7 (Cambridge: Jubilee Centre Publications, 1987), p.57.

7   See Roger Cowe and Simon Williams, *Who are the Ethical Consumers?* (Manchester: Co-operative Bank, 2000).

8   'The Illusion of Choice: disadvantaged consumers and the use of small shops', *Insight*, no.4, Aug 1993, Jubilee Policy Group, Jubilee Centre, Cambridge, UK.

9   Based on information from the American Academy of Matrimonial Lawyers. See: *www.aaml.org*.

10   Will Hutton, *Putting Back the P in PLC: public companies and a new corporate citizenship* (Industrial Society, London 2001), p.8.

11   Will Hutton, *op. cit.*, p.8. 'The Domini 400 includes companies who have a good record on the environment, product quality, community and employee relations; it has consistently outperformed the Dow and Standard & Poors since its launch in 1990 and provides the stocks for inclusion in the Domini Social Fund.'

CHAPTER SIX

LUNCH

Jack is an international estate agent based in Boston, USA. He runs his business from a ground floor suite of offices he's nicknamed the 'Bat Cave'. A former Yale footballer, he's always valued teamwork as an ingredient of business success. But as his own company expanded and diversified and took on more staff, he had to work out how to make the teamwork real:

'About ten years ago, I realised I wasn't seeing people as often as before', Jack explained. 'I was running around and so was everybody else. We never got a chance to sit down and talk.'
Jack worried about the impact of this disconnectedness of his business, in which sharing information is critical, so he started a Thursday ritual: a free pizza lunch in the office.
'I know this is not an advanced management technique', Jack said. 'On Thursdays, we sit around the big table in my office and we talk. There is no agenda. The group averages about 15 people and changes members every week, but there is a core of five or six who provide continuity. They meet even when I'm not there. We all look forward to it not as a business meeting, but as an opportunity for informal talk. People catch up with each other, they brainstorm, they bring up stuff that doesn't get discussed elsewhere. And it works.'[1]

BEYOND THURSDAY PIZZA

Traditionally, in every culture, eating and socialising are linked – and not just at lunch. Families and friends have their food-focused get-togethers at Christmas and birthdays. Lovers share their candlelit dinner. Business colleagues wrangle as they down their cappuccino and toasted ciabatta sandwich. Almost all of us meet friends for coffee, or join our mates in the pub or the wine bar.

When we eat and drink, we like company. More than that, eating and drinking with others reinforces social bonds and strengthens relationships. Literally and metaphorically, it 'brings us together'. That's why Jack used it to help build his company.

This social function of eating is broadly the same in the business and domestic arenas. In the home, however, the issues at stake may be slightly different.

To a large extent, the social group we call a household is identified by the presence of its members around the dinner table. As a base of 'plenary' rather than one-to-one communication, the shared meal provides a unique chance both to reinforce a sense of membership and to engage in forward planning.

As a relational opportunity it also carries some unusual qualities – particularly in child-raising. For instance, because there are fewer distractions, children are more likely to focus on conversation. Unlike the hour before school, interaction with parents will not be task-related, and this means children will be more likely to feel comfortable offloading problems they're going through with peers or school work.[2]

Hearing adults discuss the day's events also gives children a window on the grown-up world. It's in this processing of the day's events that your values most clearly emerge. What you did or didn't do in a given situation. What you thought of somebody else's action, and how you chose to respond to it.

Studies indicate that family meals produce long-term benefits. For example, psychologists Blake Sperry Bowden and Jennie Zeisz recently studied the link between family eating and the social problems of teens. They took a sample of 527 teenagers and categorised each one as either 'well-adjusted' or 'not well-adjusted'. The 'well-adjusted' teens (less likely to take drugs or be depressed, more motivated at school, and with better peer relationships) ate with their families an average of five days a week. The 'not well-adjusted group' ate as a family only three days.[3]

And don't forget, of course, that eating with your children lets you nag them about eating those greens – not a frivolous point, since a

Harvard Medical School survey of 16,000 nine to fourteen-year-olds found that 'kids who sit down to eat with their siblings and parents eat nearly a whole serving more of fruit or vegetables, per day, than those who rarely eat *en famille* ... communal eaters consumed more iron and vitamins B_6, B_{12}, C and E.'[4]

WHAT MICROWAVE OVENS DO TO RELATIONSHIPS

The classic family meal, though, is less common than it once was – for at least two reasons.

First, an increasing number of people – the young as well as the elderly – live on their own.[5] Inevitably, this means more meals are consumed standing in the kitchen or sitting in front of the TV.[6] If you live on your own, therefore, meals won't affect your relationships one way or the other unless you make a special effort. You either have to invite someone around, or incur the extra expense of eating out.

Second, even for those whose 'significant others' share the same household, the competing demands of work, school, friends and clubs often make it increasingly hard to use mealtimes as a way of bringing everyone together – at least for any more than ten minutes. Not surprisingly, according to research conducted for Paxo, almost a quarter of UK families don't manage to eat together even once a week.[7]

Unexpectedly, perhaps, technology seems to make this juggling of timetables even more difficult.

Food technology has kept up with – and in many ways facilitated – our changing lifestyle. We can only stagger the evening meal over two or three hours if we can serve reasonably varied and palatable food in small units – whether it's chicken tikka masala, or a tin of beans.

In this way, food technology buys us time. Like other small domestic miracles – hot plumbing, piped-in power, vacuum cleaners, washing machines – it claws back the hours we might have spent in unrewarding labour and gives them back to us to use at our discretion.

A good example is the microwave oven. The genius of the microwave is to produce a wide range of cooked foods – and to do it in about as long as it takes you to untie your shoelaces. No risky stirring of white sauce. No agonising wait. The microwave can do what even the most accomplished domestic cook cannot – turn out hot individual portions fast and efficiently and do it again and again and again.

But that's not all the microwave does. It also rearranges what we might call the 'unavoidable interactions' in the home. Buying a microwave doesn't prevent people eating together, of course. But if you can warm up macaroni cheese at seven, there's less pressure on you to get back home and share a pizza at six.

On one level, the technology is helping us cope with our time-pressured lifestyles and non-aligned schedules. On another level – and simultaneously – it is removing a reason to put relating time first.

Incidentally, the same is true of clearing away the dishes. A survey commissioned by the British supermarket giant Tesco revealed that 68 per cent of washers-up had been kissed at the kitchen sink.[8] The aphrodisiac effects of detergent? Sadly not. It just illustrates how the 'unavoidable' task of washing dishes after a meal offers an excuse to be with, and be close to, others we care about. Do we love washing up? No. Is it a good time to talk? Often, yes.

Conversation grows in this kind of soil. Sit someone down for the purpose of 'having a conversation' – and you'll produce awkwardness. Work on a joint task that removes the necessity for eye contact and gives your hands something to do – and conversation will flow naturally.

Devices like microwaves and dishwashers, then, present us with more than one set of questions. We are used to asking: How much does it cost? Have I got room for it in my kitchen? Does it fit my colour scheme? How much can I fit inside it? But it's just as reasonable to ask: What effects might the use of this machine have on relationships? Is the time spent together on household tasks more usefully spent on individual pursuits? If I buy this machine, how do I preserve household conversation?

TAKING THE R OPTION WITH LUNCH – AND OTHER MEALS

Individual practices differ a lot. However, the tradition of the convivial meal *as routine* is less deeply rooted in the USA and the UK than in, say, southern Europe. This owes something to the UK's smaller family size and greater mobility. It also reflects a difference in national culture. Visiting France, for example, it will strike many Britons and Americans how long it takes the waiter to find their table, and how little urgency the chef displays in cooking the food. We're not always ready for such generous opportunities to relate.

If eating is to provide a useful relationship opportunity, though, conviviality must be part of the mix. And within and around the busy corporate world, this often requires forethought and planning.

1. Use lunch at work to build relationships with colleagues

The office lunch is more than the equivalent of popping out onto the balcony to smoke a cigarette. A recent report by the Industrial Society in the UK has drawn attention to the way relationship-building benefits productivity.

According to the report's author, Judith Doyle, 'Employers should give their staff more room to enjoy their work. Instead of seeing sociability at work as the antithesis to efficiency and productivity, they should see it as crucial to the bottom line.'

She goes on: 'Gossip is the cement which holds organisations together. Providing communal space such as coffee areas or lunchroom, allows employees to share information, knowledge and build relations that benefit both company and the employee.'[9]

In other words, there are some good reasons not to phone for a sandwich and stay at your desk. The rhythm lunch-breaks bestow on the working day, and the opportunities they create for building work relationships, are worth making time for.

2. Making corporate hospitality work

Of course, there are many occasions when social eating is deliberately harnessed in the quest to create new business with people outside the company. It may be worth reflecting, then, on what you are trying to achieve in relationship terms by laying on corporate hospitality – whether it's a simple meal out, or some more elaborate form of entertaining.

Corporate hospitality is not, fundamentally, about trying to impress visiting executives by giving them a good time. Relaxing together will usually tend to 'warm people up'. But that isn't the final goal. You are using corporate hospitality with the aim of building relationships at their various stages – wooing, initiating, developing, cementing, deepening or celebrating.

In relational terms, corporate hospitality works because it encourages face-to-face contact, opens up non-task-related time, and promotes a more open agenda. These qualities help you in three ways.

First, you can gain a broader knowledge of the company or department you are dealing with. The informal meeting allows conversation to range over 'irrelevant' topics which may nevertheless reveal new areas of opportunity or correct flawed and potentially damaging assumptions.

Second, you get a broader knowledge of the individuals you are dealing with – their values, experience, skills and roles, as well as the pressures and constraints they work under. This allows you to identify potential contributions and initiatives that would not exist with a different set of people. And it gives you a fund of conversational openers to keep relationships 'on track' in future communication by email or phone.

Third, the face-to-face element will always provide the opportunity of building trust, understanding, and personal commitment. You can show respect for, and interest in, the person you are dealing with. In short, you can lay the foundation not just of a business relationship, but of a real friendship.

Despite all this, much corporate hospitality is still planned on a formulaic basis – that is, without thinking through what might be achieved. Given the amount of time and money invested, this is surprising. One way to benefit from taking the R option, then, is to ask how the structuring of a hospitality event is likely to affect relational outcomes.

For example, is there the right balance between entertainment (the game, the theatre) and opportunities to relate one-to-one? Are you planning the important relating-times at points where people will be fresh and rested? And are you showing hospitality to the right people?

Customers, suppliers, strategic partners, investors and staff are all key to business success. If your business relationships are the source of your profitability, well-thought-through corporate hospitality should be a vital part of your comprehensive strategy for maintaining those relationships.[10]

3. Togetherness matters more than formalities

As far as we (Michael and David) are concerned, neither of us have ever been one for the theatrics of dinner parties. We'd much rather invite people into the kitchen and throw them a vegetable peeler than usher them into a candlelit dining room with a glass of sherry. The reason, we think, is that we see the dinner party as a time to get alongside people.

After all, a meal involves a collection of activities surrounding the preparation and eating of food. From a relational viewpoint, it's successful even if your prize soufflé sinks – so long as people connect in conversation. And the same applies in ordinary domestic eating. People in a family or sharing a flat should be able – even if only once a week – to share the cooking and muck in with the washing up. If your kitchen's large enough, it can easily become the social centre of the house – a place where people will hang around rather than disappearing to their own rooms.

4. Set the interaction rules

Just like any other area of life, meals can be an arena for bad relating. In households, particularly, people drag to the dinner table much of the emotional baggage of their day. Which may mean you'll want to think through in advance the kinds of interaction that are likely to take place.

Fairly obviously, it helps conversation if you are sitting around a table facing one another. Yes, watching the news can be educational, but in relationship terms having the TV on at mealtimes can easily represent a wasted opportunity.

In family situations it's worth remembering that, as an adult, you set the rules and act as the chairperson. A few clear rules judiciously enforced will help children both to relate well and to absorb the basics of politeness. Make your requirements fair and they will tend to stick.

But children won't relax if you're too picky with them. Most family therapists will tell you that meals are not a good occasion to bring up disciplinary matters or uncompleted homework – not least because this 'public' setting will produce shaming rather than creative motivation.

Consider turning off the mobile and turning on the answering machine – moves that will not only save you from distractions but demonstrate clearly how you value and prioritise mealtimes. And if people have a habit of not turning up when you call them, try ringing a bell. Yelling up the stairs is hard on the voice and tends to start things off on a sour note.

5. Ring-fence mealtimes

Finding – and protecting – time for shared meals takes real effort. Twenty minutes isn't enough. You need a period long enough to unwind from the tensions of the day – a period in which everyone can feel there is nothing more pressing to do than be in the kitchen and enjoy each other's company. Difficult? Of course. But if relationships matter, it comes down to priorities.

We all face huge competition for time. Adults get back late from work. There's homework to be done. Somebody will have an absolutely must-see TV programme. On Tuesdays, somebody else will be out till eight at a gymnastics class. And so it goes on.

But again, if mealtimes matter, the R option must be negotiated fairly and firmly to ensure they are protected on at least a reasonable number of days each week. Find the best-fit solution that's fair all round. And compromise creatively. If dinner's impossible, consider making an occasion of breakfast. The North American tradition of weekend pancakes and syrup – at home or out – has something going for it.

6. Make sure there's something to talk about

A senior executive once said to me (Michael), 'You know, I would never go to a board meeting without spending several hours reading the papers carefully, and thinking through what I'm going to say.' If you pressed me, I would have to say that I regard the time that I spent with my teenagers over dinner as more significant from a long-term point of view than any board meeting. However, I spent no time at all thinking through in advance what we would discuss over dinner, and no time reflecting afterwards about who said what around the table.

Indeed, I believe that my daughter, our youngest child, suffered to some degree as a consequence of this neglect. Her two older brothers held the floor too often, and for too long, so she seldom got a chance to express her point of view. Although my daughter is now more than adequately articulate, I wish that I had given her greater opportunity to make her contribution at family mealtimes.

Am I not right? In business, we routinely lay out agendas and guide discussions. Yet in the personal arena we let conversation proceed in a haphazard manner, with no particular objective in mind. If we go to the trouble of creating shared time together over a meal, it stands to reason that we will want to use that time well. And good conversation doesn't just spring out of the air.

Well-conducted conversation helps children to talk, builds confidence, and teaches them to listen well. It tells parents what children are thinking and worrying about. One of the most important qualities you can bring to the discussion is a clear interest in what another person has to say. It's the failure of adults to take a real interest in their children's worlds that makes the two groups end up with so little to say to each other.

One seventeen-year-old sees clearly what's going on across the generation gap:

> Dad never really listens. Mum has to take centre-stage without being interrupted. I think it's legitimate to interrupt: it shows interest. It's better with my friends because they treat me as a peer, and they get impassioned about things, which parents don't. A conversation should be fuelled by the passion that we have for the subject.[11]

Family conversations have a habit of becoming self-fuelling if you can only get them off the launch pad. Really almost anything will do as a starter, provided it engages interest and doesn't make people feel they're being interrogated. Ask people around the table what they like or detest. What they'd do if they had a million pounds. Whether they think it's a good idea to buy a chimpanzee as a pet.

7. Bring in the outside

Conversation can become inbred. So there's a world of difference between families who regard themselves as havens from the outside world, and families that see the outside world as a beach to be combed for exciting and valuable new experience.

Variety enlivens interaction. People can 'dine out' on a good story because what they have to say transports their listeners into unknown places, arouses curiosity, sparks imagination. Theodore Zeldin, a passionate exponent of the art of conversation, believes that 'humanity is a family which has hardly met. One of the best ways it can meet is for our traditions of family hospitality to be revived.'

And if you can't bring newcomers in, let the novelty of the world be transmitted through the excursions of family members. The family, says Zeldin,

> ... may treat itself as a base from which its members set out to explore the outside world, and to which they return with something new to say, so that conversation is constantly enriched by outside as well as inside happenings ... It is by conversations with others, by mixing different voices with our own, that we can turn our individual life into an original work of art.[12]

8. Read the meeting

Looking back, I (Michael) can see that my senior executive friend was right, too, in pointing out the importance of review. Be aware of dynamics – especially the dynamics that aren't being expressed. I can't remember how many times I've shared a table with my three children, and I always assumed the meals were a positive experience for everyone. It took me years to realise what should have been obvious if I'd bothered to check it. As I mentioned earlier, most of the conversation was carried by the two witty, articulate, and older boys. My daughter, the youngest child, often didn't get a look-in. Thinking back, I could have managed those mealtime conversations much better than I did. But I didn't read them.

---

1   Reported by Edward M. Hallowell, 'The Human Moment at Work,' *Harvard Business Review,* January–February, 1999.
2   This assumes, of course, that the television is off. Almost 50% of respondents to a survey said they balanced dinner on their laps while watching television, and only

45% said they chatted around the table. 'Television shatters dinner chatter' by Stuart Millar, *The Guardian*, 29 September 1997, p.5.

3   See *APA Monitor,* 28 (10), 8, (October 1997).

4   M. W. Gillman, S. L. Rifas-Shiman, *et al,* 'Family dinner and diet duality among older children and adolescents', *Archives of Family Medicine* 9, 235–240 (2000).

5   The proportion of one-person households in the UK is 12%, compared with 15% in Germany and 24% in Sweden. (Source: Eurostat). As for the USA, in 1900 only 5% of households consisted of one person, whereas 20% contained seven or more. Today this situation has reversed. In 1998, 26% of American households contained a single person. Source: US census statistics. See www.census.gov

6   Note that in 1998 the UK food retailer Tesco saw a 63% increase in sales of meals for one. Reported in the *Birmingham Post,* 18 January, 1999.

7   See *Daily Telegraph,* 3 April 2001.

8   Cited by Virginia Ironside, *Independent,* 27 October 1995.

9   Industrial Society, *New Community or New Slavery? The Emotional Division of Labour* (published 22 November 2000).

10 John Ashcroft, 'Corporate Hospitality', unpublished paper, November 1998, the Relationships Foundation.

11 Quoted by Theodore Zeldin, *Conversation* (London: Harvill Press, 1998), p.33.

12 Theodore Zeldin, *op.cit.,* p.46.

CHAPTER SEVEN

LEISURE

For sheer architectural splendour, London's Bluewater Shopping Centre doesn't quite rank alongside Notre Dame – though it does have particularly luxurious toilets.

From the moment you leave your car in one of the 130,000 parking spaces, you know that this colossal blend of retailing and leisure puts you, the consumer, bang in the middle of the frame. As the developers say:

> The guests' experience has been enhanced by creating a sense of place including cultural elements and civic art, by creating attractive environments in which to eat and relax, by including internal and external landscapes, and redefining customer services and amenities.[1]

If nothing else, the arrival of giant indoor malls in Britain shows that leisure is big business – something large numbers of people spend large amounts of money on. But as a consumer, you find yourself pulled in two very different directions.

It's clear that shopping in the mega-mall is understood to be a *social* activity. People go there with friends or family. Many of them are wearing their best outfits. And the whole place has clearly been designed to encourage those positive emotions we associate with good company.

At the same time, however, Bluewater belongs to a commercial culture in which recreation of all kinds is tending to focus more and more on *individual* fulfilment.

Almost everything you might do in your time off – from embroidery to extreme sports – has generated a range of accessories. Is cycling your bag? Then don't just buy a bike and helmet. Try on the shorts.

Check out the shades. Save your lungs with a mask. Get a whistle to warn off errant pedestrians.

THE PROBLEM OF LIVING IN A WORLD OF YOUR OWN

To some extent, all this is a side effect of increasing wealth. We now demand and expect that our individual preferences should be catered for. We want an exact fit. I buy a snowboard, you buy skis. Also, as technologies get cheaper, it becomes possible for individuals to buy, for personal use, equipment they'd previously have shared.

A 1999 survey commissioned by Avis Car Rental reported that 40 per cent of British drivers normally drive alone.[2] Mobile phone use in the UK is expanding so fast that any figure you put on it is instantly out of date. Two in every three British children have a TV in their bedroom, including half of six- and seven-year-olds.[3]

On the positive side, you can say that this development gives you greater individual control and thus greater individual satisfaction. Also, individually controlled technologies like text messaging have some relational benefits.[4] But there's a negative side too. Because the more you grow accustomed to entertaining yourself in solitude, the less effort you will put into making and sustaining relationships.

In a recent survey, roughly 4,000 American adults from 3,000 households reported that, since going online, they spent eight per cent less time attending social events, 13 per cent less time with family and friends, and 26 per cent less time talking to people on the phone. Those who spent five to ten hours a week online reported a 25 per cent fall in social activity. They said they 'see fewer people, talk to fewer people, and go out less often'.[5]

This isn't an argument against Internet use. But if time is the currency of relationships, then the way we redeploy our time to accommodate new technologies is an issue deserving thought. Not only do unsocial hours make our leisure periods less likely to coincide; we are also tending to give a larger slice of our discretionary time to solo activities.

It's illuminating to see what happens when you try to reverse the pattern. For example, as research for a newspaper feature, reporter Diane Appleyard went cold turkey on technology – in this case, by locking up the family television for a week. The effects surprised her – and illustrate what kind of trade-offs occur when you try to organise your life differently:

> By the end of the TV-free week, I noticed a marked improvement in the children's attitude to each other and to me. It made them use their imagination to create fantasy games, such as dens. Beth read four books in the course of the week. Charlotte learned several new card games, and we read lots of books together.
>
> The house, however, is a tip. No TV means playing games and creating mess. I am also exhausted. The week made me realise how much I rely on the TV to get them out of my hair. It is the literal equivalent of being able to put them both in a cupboard for a couple of hours, and presumably just as stimulating.[6]

FILLING THE SPACE WHEN PEOPLE AREN'T THERE

When I (David) switch on the radio news in the morning, I suddenly feel a part of that loose network of relationships that constitutes my citizenship of the world. Like TV and the Internet, radio is an information service connecting me to events in government, society, industry, and the markets. I don't need to know anyone in the studio, and they certainly don't need to know me. To eavesdrop on the national gossip is enough.

On other kinds of radio, though, quite a different thing happens. Driving down the M1 late one night, I listened to an abrasive talk-radio DJ fielding calls at random from anyone who cared to pick up a phone. Here the wider world was irrelevant. The main business to hand was between the DJ and the lonely, bored, sometimes desperate people for whom he seemed to have become (for want of a better term) a significant social contact.

It's a peculiarity of our media-intense culture that we can enjoy an imagined intimacy with complete strangers. Presenters on both TV and radio affect a personal manner, which suggests that the illusion of relationship matters to the media-user's sense of inclusion in the wider community. It could be argued, in fact, that the media in general provides us with a set of 'surrogate family members' – celebrities we all feel we know, and in whose stories we all have an interest.

It's for this reason, presumably, that crowds of complete strangers register grief when media personalities die (British broadcaster Jill Dando, for example, or the Princess of Wales).[7] They've even been known to send flowers to television studios when familiar TV soap characters pass away.

We are not disparaging the role of TV or radio as a social companion, or as a means of providing entertainment, education or raised social awareness. Where real human relationships are lacking, the media's ability to mimic intimacy can perform an important role. But media intimacy is still an illusion. And if it weans us away from real, human intimacies, it may, paradoxically, end up deepening our isolation.

TAKING THE R OPTION IN LEISURE

Recreation is an opportunity. It's time you can use as you wish. If you're a working parent, you may have less free time than you want, and the way you use it may have to take account of other people's needs. Conversely, if you're retired, or unemployed, you may have *more* free time than you want. Either way, if you want to take the R option seriously, free time is a key resource. You only get to live each day once.

1. Look at activities in terms of their relational value

Clearly some activities – including most sports – are inherently social. You can't play football on your own. That said, different issues arise depending on whether you play for your company team (thus reinforcing work relationships) or play for a side whose other members you're unlikely to see except out on the field.

But there's more to this than favouring bridge over solitaire. For example, take the much argued-over issue of television. It's true that on average we watch a huge amount of TV,[8] and that communication between household members usually diminishes when the TV is on. But then the same criticism – in essence, that solitary pursuits cause social damage – can be made of reading books.

Books, of course, enjoy favoured status. They're like spinach – something generally agreed to be 'good for you'. That, though, isn't really the point. What matters is how far your solitary activity feeds your interaction at other times. For everybody to watch the cup final or superbowl, or the latest costume drama, or even the latest tragic twist in *EastEnders*, has relational value if it becomes grist in the mill of tomorrow's conversation.

This is one reason, incidentally, why the proliferation of channels, and the use of pay channels, may not be helpful for relationships. Clearly, having a single state-run channel can be stultifying and open to abuse by manipulation. But beyond a certain point, the more we get to pick our own viewing material, the less immediate shared experience we have as a basis for conversation.

There's also the matter of using activities to draw in other people. You can walk on your own, or you can walk in company. You can wash your car at the filling station, or you can wash it yourself out on the street where you get interrupted by talkative neighbours and inquisitive children.

In this sense, pets count as a leisure activity. A dog in a family is a kind of dummy contributor – a catalyst, provoking action and interaction, and a symbolic device, providing a conversational starter with other dog-walkers. It becomes an intermittent focus of attention and conversation. And like a child, it has the ability to interrupt and surprise. Try as you may, you won't get that kind of relational input from your cyberpet.

2. Think about the way you use holiday time

In relationship terms, large blocks of free time are a bit like large lump sums of cash. You have to decide how to spend them.

For centuries, our dependence on natural light and the influence of a broadly Christian culture have kept us relaxing after dark and on Sundays. These boundaries have recently begun to break down. One positive result is greater individual convenience – being able to work late and pick up a pint of milk at the supermarket at four in the morning.

But this drift to unsocial hours and the much-vaunted 24-hour society also has the effect of dislocating us socially. Our schedules get out of synch. It gets harder to meet friends and family at a mutually convenient time. Particularly within the family, therefore, making free time coincide can become a lifeline for keeping relationships healthy.

Sundays are surprisingly important here. After all, if you live to be seventy, Sundays will have taken up ten years of your life. Nine million people in Britain now work 'sometimes or regularly' on Sundays.[9] For all of these individuals and their close friends and relatives, there may be no single day of the week when they are able to spend time together. It is a particular problem for households with school age children, and even more so where the parent working on Sunday is also working on Saturday – surely an issue in the debate surrounding the quality of parenting.

It's also worth thinking about how you use annual leave. Though the brochures seldom say it outright, holidays aren't just about seeing new things, eating exotic foods, or lying on a warm, remote beach. The fourteen days you spend on vacation are one of your most valuable relating opportunities.

So who do you go with? Taking a tour with strangers is, of course, a good way of 'meeting people', especially for singles with room in their lives to make new friends and keep up with them. Alternatively, the institution of the 'family holiday' provides a means of building up *existing* relationships. For two weeks, the nuclear family group gets to spend recreational time together in a setting more stimulating and relaxed than the working week at home.

But even here, it's worth thinking through the details. Which relationships are most needing time? It may be a relief for mum and dad to offload the kids onto the hotel children's club – but is that helping you relate as a family? Presumably, you don't want to get back from Tenerife and find your children remembering more about the club leader than they remember about you. And how do you use the time with your partner when the kids are off at their beach volleyball lessons? Is it time used in building your relationship, or time spent sunbathing?

These issues become more complex in reconstituted families. If partners no longer live together, or if there are fresh partners and new combinations of children, the question of who you spend your valuable holiday time with becomes both more urgent and tougher to answer.

Of course, you don't have to take your holiday off-the-peg. It's possible, for example, to use holiday time for visiting family and friends rather than isolating yourselves on a distant beach. It's possible to team up with friends. And it's possible to go on a retreat and spend the time completely alone – giving you future relational benefits through being able to recuperate and 'recharge your batteries'.

3. Concentrate when relating

Much as it pains me to admit it, I (David) am not a natural with children. In part, I think, this has to do with the male passion for completing tasks and achieving results. In part it simply follows from the pressures of work. I sometimes find myself with one eye on the game I'm playing, and the other on the clock.

I recognise this as a weakness. Work will still be around in twenty years' time – but the children will not. For their sake and for mine, it's worth making the effort not only to spend time with them, but to give them my whole, undivided, and unconditional attention. Even if that means playing a meandering child-led game with dolls rather than a focused and task-oriented project involving a construction toy.

The problems men have in relating to women have been well documented. Typically, in a close relationship, the man will think the woman talks too much and the woman will think she's not being listened to. Learning to concentrate when relating to a female partner, and learning to sympathise without jumping in with solutions, is an art most men seem curiously unable to master.[10]

4. Communicate for recreation

Not many of us would list 'conversation' among our hobbies and interests. Next to white-water rafting, it sounds a bit tame. Nevertheless, getting to know others must count among the most enriching experiences life has to offer – and for this, conversation is the key.

Men, particularly, are better at swapping facts than they are at the intricate art of communication. Conversing, debating, letter writing, sharing feelings and perceptions as well as facts – these are relational skills to which many of us give insufficient attention. Yet living in an age of communications makes them more – not less – important.

Busy people have a tendency to fall back on the Christmas card list when there's not time to sustain a relationship in person or by phone. Stuffing the annual 'family news sheet' into the envelope, however, is a poor substitute for direct interaction. For one thing, the sheet simply contains information. For another, you may often be sending more information than many want to receive.

In the matter of keeping people informed, more creative use might be made of family websites and executive summaries. On a website you can more easily and cheaply include photographs, and provide up-to-date details on how to reach you by other means. Otherwise – why not bite the bullet and make a phone call?

---

1   Taken from Bluewater's website at www.bluewater.co.uk
2   Avis Car Rental, *Will Travel in Britain Ever Change? A Report on Attitudes Towards the Car and Alternative Transport Solutions*, 9 June 1999.
3   Sonia Livingstone and Moira Bovill, 'Young People, New Media: Press release' (Available online at http://lito.lse.ac.uk/young-people/press.html), London School of Economics and Political Science, 18 March 1999. The project was funded by the Advertising Association, the BBC, BT plc, the Broadcasting Standards Commission, the European Commission (DGXII), the European Parliament, the European Science Foundation, the ITV Network Centre, the Independent Television Commission, the Leverhulme Trust, STICERD LSE and Yorkshire/Tyne Tees Television.

   The study looked at the use of TV, video, books, computer games, music and personal computers in the UK. It found that young people use the media for around five hours each day and points to the dominance within the UK of 'screen-entertainment culture.' Television occupies about half of this time and is named as the medium which young people 'would miss most'.
4   19% of 15 to 24-year-old users in the UK have sent a text message to ask someone out on a date, 49% have invited someone to a party with a text message, 44% have apologised after an argument via a text message. Note also, however, that 13% have sent a text message to end a relationship. MORI Polls & Surveys, I Just Text to Say I Love You, 5 September 2000. On:
      http://www.mori.com/polls/2000/lycos.shtml
5   Figures from the Stanford Institute for the Quantitative Study of Society in America. See Cherry Norton, 'Even moderate surfing harms your social life,' *Independent,* 28 February 2000.
6   Diane Appleyard, 'TV Cold Turkey,' *FEMAIL Forum (Daily Mail),* 17 December 1998.
7   There are still web pages commemorating Diana's death. One, put up by a family in Africa, has animated candles burning and proclaims: 'We maintain this page as a memorial in her honour.'

8 In the UK, the average number of hours per week spent watching television by people over the age of 4 is 24.1 for males and 26.9 for females (Social Trends 2001, table 13.3, p.225). In the USA, the Social Capital Community Benchmark Survey records an average of 3.8 hours per weekday
(http://www.cfsv.org/communitysurvey/docs/marginals.pdf).

9 Source: *Labour Force Survey, Great Britain, 1992, 1998*, as cited in G. Watson (1993) 'Sunday Working in Britain' in Employment Gazette, Vol.101, No.11, pp.503–14, and Hill, R. & Dex, S. 'The Business and Family Consequences of Deregulating Sunday Trading in Britain', Judge Institute for Management Studies, Working Paper Series, unpublished, 1999.

10 Some of the issues in communication between men and women have been treated helpfully by John Gray's *Men are from Mars, Women are from Venus* (London: HarperCollins, 1992).

CHAPTER EIGHT

FRIENDS

In 1985, the Irish academic Brian Keenan left Belfast to take up a position at the American University of Beirut. Not long after he'd arrived, a Mercedes pulled up beside him in a back alley and four armed Shi'ite militiamen forced him inside. It was the beginning of a four-and-a-half-year ordeal.

For Keenan – who tells the story memorably – the saving grace lay in the friendship he formed with fellow captive, John McCarthy. Keenan and McCarthy, working-class Irish socialist and English public school-educated journalist, could hardly have been more different. And yet Keenan would make this comment about the final moment of his release:

I remember every moment of my time alone, my time with John and with those other captives. And I remember how we first met, our relationship, the kinds of needs I had of John and he of me. And how we sought always to give and take, thinking always of each other. And as I review it all, all the wonder, I see his face stare at mine. I had watched this man grow, become full and in his fullness enrich me.[1]

Sharing a mattress in a cramped, dark basement is hardly a circumstance you'd expect to foster friendship. Yet the bond that formed between them had the same two sources as friendships that arise in far more ordinary situations – the sources of *common ground* and *enjoyment.*

In the first instance, their common ground consisted of little more than a shared pain. But it had the required effect. In more comfortable surroundings – say, seated next to each other on a long-haul flight – they might never have got beyond a few words of polite small talk.

Common ground assures you that you somehow 'belong to the same group' and therefore have something to say to one another. It crops up through overlaps in experience or social background or political outlook, and through shared workplaces, sports clubs and self-help groups like Alcoholics Anonymous. Much common ground arises through family connections – both in the sense of belonging to the same family and of sharing the experience of being a parent or a grandparent.

It's not always obvious that two individuals have something in common. One of my (Michael's) wife's friends of many years could hardly have been more different from her. My wife lives in middle-class suburban Cambridge; her friend spent her days – and often nights – working among the homeless at London's King's Cross. Yet they were drawn to one another through a shared sense of dissatisfaction with the status quo.

Common ground is widely used as a criterion for starting and pursuing a friendship. When you identify another person as 'your type' you are responding to unspoken signals in dress or manner or style that reassure you that this other person is a member of your particular tribe. On the same basis, you will tend to 'screen out' people who don't appear to conform to the norms you feel comfortable with.

But not all common ground produces friendships. The process of friendship only gets started, and only leads to bonding, if two people discover that they enjoy one another's company enough to commit time to shared activity. By enjoyment, we mean, broadly, the deriving of benefits from a friend's company. This includes a number of things. For example:

- Simply having fun.

- The sense of being valued by another person for your own sake – and not for your connections or status or skills.

- Having someone to listen to you when you need to talk.

- Knowing a friend will always sympathise, accept you and stand by you rather than pass judgement.

- Knowing a friend can be trusted with intimacies.

- Having a concerned outside voice to advise you.

Where there is no enjoyment, a relationship remains merely functional, as between work colleagues. But where common ground exists, and two people begin to derive benefits of enjoyment from the relationship, it will become part of the relational base discussed in the chapter on roots – part of your support network.

The friendship process is not one-size-fits-all. It reaches many levels, from congenial acquaintance to strong dependency. You may feel you need many friends, or only one, depending on your character and circumstances. The felt need for friendship also varies over time, tending to be greater when you are young and unattached, or elderly and in danger of becoming socially isolated.

Note also that the friendship process can lapse or go into reverse if either of the sources of friendship – common ground or enjoyment – is lost. Friendship is, in sociology-speak, very context-dependent – that is, it often rests on circumstances that bring people together and give them opportunities and motives to relate. If those circumstances change, as they generally do when you leave university, move house, or change jobs, many friendships will fade, making room for new ones. 'While cultural this is sometimes interpreted as an indication that the relationship was somehow deficient ... in reality it is an entirely routine and unexceptional process.'[2]

This common experience of 'drifting apart' doesn't damage the friendship per se – only prevents it from being pursued. Meet an old friend, and it's surprising how quickly you'll 'pick up where you left off', so long as the friendship had strong foundations.

By contrast, if the integrity of the friendship itself is challenged – through actions like betrayal or the breaking of confidences – enjoyment is lost, and one party may deliberately withdraw, perhaps leaving the friendship irreparably broken. A study of lost friendships found that a 'major factor was breaking certain rules, especially "third-party" rules, about keeping confidences, standing up for friends in their absence, and being jealous of other relationships'.[3]

FRIENDS AND SOUL MATES

There is a convention in the wording of personal ads that runs something like this: 'Person A (with certain named attributes), wltm

Person B (with certain named attributes), *for friendship and maybe more.'*

There are variations: 'would-like-to-meet for friendship/relationship,' or 'for friendship, possibly romance'. What's striking is how frequently the advertisers employ the idea of friendship as a kind of 'first base', and how, also, they appear to see friendship merely as a step towards something else.

It's often said – and with some truth – that marriages or long-term partnerships succeed if the partners are also friends. The sources of friendship – common ground and enjoyment – inevitably play a strong part in maintaining partnerships, unless the link is principally an economic one. Nevertheless, since the time of the ancient Greeks, a sharp distinction has been recognised between the process of friendship and the process of romantic attachment, and thus between the status of friend and that of 'soul mate'.

The distinction comes down to two issues.

First, the lover is an object of desire in a way the friend is not. True, friendship can be intense. Brian Keenan, for example, did not shrink from using the term 'love' to describe his relationship with McCarthy. But the exceptional depth of intimacy between them was not arrived at by way of erotic desire. Friends who have become lovers will recognise the clear shift in register that occurred when they went beyond simply enjoying each other's company and became deeply absorbed in one another. At that point, overtones of exclusiveness, possessiveness and self-abandonment enter into the relationship – overtones not characteristic of a relationship between friends.

Second, discovering that someone is your soul mate rather than simply your friend usually makes you want to erect some flags around the relationship to mark it as a permanent feature of your life. The reasons why this instinct is sound are examined further in the chapter on soul mates. For now, we are only noting that this rendering of desire into public commitment is not characteristic of friendship. Friends don't formally sign up for the relationship. In fact the essence of friendship is that either party remains free to withdraw.[4]

Once you've made a commitment to a soul mate, however, and assuming you meant it, certain consequences will follow for your relationships with friends. For example, since you only have so much 'disposable time' in the week, you are likely to prioritise your central relationship over others – a move which can sometimes cause mis-understanding. Also, if you regard sexual passion as belonging exclusively to your relationship with your soul mate, other relationships with sexual potential will need careful handling.

FRIENDSHIPS WHERE YOU WORK

Alongside leisure activities, workplaces are often the richest source of friendship, furnishing common ground in the form of shared space, shared goals, and shared gripes. Some recent changes in the Western workplace have encouraged this – notably the shift away from noisy machine-based manufacturing to service industry, office work and more relationship-intensive work practices. Not all the changes have benefited friendship. Teleworking, for example, can make forming and maintaining work friendships much more difficult.

Friendship between employees undoubtedly delivers benefits to the firm, partly because friendship is the basis of effective team-bonding. Not surprisingly, therefore, studies have shown that employees who establish close relationships in 'downtime' – playing games, teasing, telling jokes over coffee – will usually also be found co-operating over work and thus boosting productivity.[5]

In some situations, individual friendships in the workplace can become problematic if they create conflicts of loyalty or a suspicion of preferential treatment. For this reason, most managers will recognise a need to balance friendship with an ethic of professionalism – in effect, a requirement that they treat all employees impartially.

In a wider context, the workplace can also pose challenges if you have a soul mate as well as friends. Office affairs are common because of the peculiar features of the workplace as a social environment.[6] For one thing, even if you have a partner, you appear at work as a single individual. It's easy for a colleague to imagine that your partner doesn't exist. Conveniently, alongside this 'assumed singleness', work also provides opportunities for intimacy – lunches, business trips, after-hours drinks – that can put extra pressure on your ability to stick to previous commitments.

TAKING THE R OPTION WITH FRIENDS

On the face of it, friendship is so intrinsically relational that there might seem little to say about an R option with friends. Often, though, we don't follow the friendship process far beyond its beginnings. Under the pressures of work and family life, friendships can get squeezed out, or redefined as leisure acquaintances that we enjoy but are unable to develop in depth. Keenan's friendship with McCarthy in Beirut cannot be treated as an ideal, still less as a norm. But it does show where the friendship process can get to if it's given enough room.

What follows isn't a complete guide to making friends, but it deals with some ways of prioritising friendship effectively and dealing with the pressure professional life can exert on our socialising.

1. Don't befriend only your clones

Because life throws so many relationships at us − not all of them wanted − we are forced to make decisions about whom we will befriend. Mostly, we don't put much thought into it. The people we get along with turn into our friends; those we don't get along with remain our acquaintances.

This can have the effect of bringing us close to those we most resemble. In thinking through the R option for friendship, though, there's something to be said for being open to friendship outside of our 'comfort zone'. Some of the greatest rewards of friendship derive from the ways in which you and your friends differ.

In the long run, you learn more, and are more enriched, by those whose outlook and experience may be vastly different from your own. You may want to ask yourself, then, how far your network extends, and whether it includes those of different ages, different cultural backgrounds, different occupations.

2. Use technology to keep up

Twenty years ago, when my wife and I (Michael) came to Cambridge after living in Africa, we had some difficulty connecting socially. One of the main reasons was the number of relatives we had elsewhere in the country. We spent many of our weekends travelling to make family visits – with the result that we didn't have much time to develop new friendships in the place where we now lived. It took a conscious reassessment to turn that around.

Today, the problem might not have been quite as acute. New jobs and new neighbourhoods demand attention, and to a certain extent the need to reallocate your time results in a 'shaking out' of your circle of friends. But it's increasingly easy for separated friends to keep in touch by phone and email. Friendships represent a big investment. You wouldn't leave money behind. Why be ready to abandon close friends simply because you've moved to a different place?

One way of taking the R option with friends, then, is to make an effort to keep up with people who matter. Try not to waste the 'bonding' experiences of working in the same firm or going to the same school or university. It's also worth using your house as a hotel. Old friends may come and spend some holiday time with you if they know there's a spare bed in your house.

3. Go beyond one-dimensional friendship

Few things stimulate friendship like a change of scene. One researcher who did some of the spadework for this book told us that she used to work for a company leading tours in Mexico. She was living in Spain at the time, and it wasn't until she invited her manager to stay in Spain that she got to know her as a friend. The difference? Simply seeing the person in a different setting. The holiday benefited both their relationship and the quality of their work when they returned to Mexico.

You don't have to travel across half the world to achieve this effect. Seeing a work friend away from work introduces all kinds of new levels into the relationship. You meet that person's other friends. You find out what drives the person in a different setting. And you end up with much more to talk about.

4. Keep it on the level

Friends, the writer C. S. Lewis once said, 'meet like sovereign princes of independent states, abroad, on neutral ground, freed from their contexts'.[7]

The notion underlying this is one of parity – of neither side feeling at a disadvantage. Contexts sometimes make parity difficult to achieve. It can be hard, for instance, to be friends with someone who is also your boss.

A respondent in a recent survey on friendship and work recalled the change that occurred when her friend at work gained promotion:

> *I can't accept the fact that she's in a supervisory role... We've just been equal for so long... When I sit there and watch her sign my time sheet, I feel ill.*[8]

There are many other ways in which parity can be disturbed. One side can be wealthier than the other, or more intellectually gifted, or more able-bodied, or better looking, or just older and more experienced. None of these differences is fatal to friendship. But to the extent that these qualities are valued and sought-after, they have a tendency to generate feelings that impede the friendship process – feelings like awe, embarrassment, self-consciousness or shame. It's just a fact that stars don't easily form friendships with fans, nor postgraduates with the illiterate.

Setting the friendship process free of these distortions may require a conscious effort to downplay differences – for example, by meeting in contexts where they are less obvious or less likely to be reinforced by other people's expectations. If one person has a well-paying job, and the other is unemployed, questions of where to meet and who pays for a drink will have a direct impact on the relationship.

Parity of input also matters. Friendships tend to go downhill if one person is left to do all the pushing – for instance by making arrangements to meet. Parity is also disturbed if one side consistently uses the other as a source of favours or as an emotional dumping-ground. The exchange of gifts and favours is essential to friendship – but it must be an exchange. In that sense, friendship involves an unspoken contract. We can break the contract both by asking too much (for example, expecting the other person to pay our way) and by asking too little (for instance, by constantly handing out advice and refusing to take any).

5. Depth matters

Studies on the link between friendship and mental health generally draw a distinction between the amount and quality of social contact. According to Michael Argyle:

Some individuals who say they are lonely actually spend as much time with friends as others; the problem can be that they do not talk about sufficiently intimate topics with them: there is insufficient self-disclosure. Some do not understand what friendship is about, that it requires concern for the other's welfare, loyalty and commitment.[9]

From time to time, everyone needs somebody they can 'offload on'. But not all friendships are substantial enough to bear this. Friendships capable of providing support in time of need are friendships where both sides are used to talking about life's more challenging issues. There has to be a certain level of self-awareness to make this work – a willingness to acknowledge and engage with your own deeper feelings. There also has to be a track record of trust – particularly if bad experiences in the past have trained you to fear hurt, misunderstanding, ridicule and rejection.

Settings can have an important influence here. Some years ago, a friend and I (David) would meet in the local steam bath. This is, I grant you, not everyone's cup of tea. But it was very relaxing; it took around three hours; and because of the deadening effect of steam on sound, it provided enough privacy to open up the sort of topics you wouldn't get talking about in the local pub.

---

1   Brian Keenan, *An Evil Cradling* (London: Random House, 1993), p.292.
2   Graham Allan, 'Social Structure and Relationships,' in Steve Duck (ed.), *Social Context and Relationships* (California: Sage, 1993), p.7.
3   See: Michael Argyle, 'The effects of relationships on wellbeing,' in Nicola Baker (ed.), *Building a Relational Society* (Aldershot: Arena, 1996), p.40.
4   Interestingly, one result of this is that people in marriages sometimes take each other for granted because the marriage has a legal existence separate from their efforts to maintain it as a living relationship.
5   See: Michael Argyle, *op.cit.*, p.41.
6   A 1990s survey by the American Management Association discovered a quarter of 500 managers interviewed said that they had experienced an office romance. Of

these, a third of men said it was with a subordinate. Additional relationship problems associated with office romance include favouritism and the increasing incidence of sexual harassment suits filed after break-up. Reported in *Global Assignment: Americans Abroad,* http://www.globalassignment.com/11-01-00/home.html

7   C. S. Lewis, *The Four Loves* (London: Fontana, 1960), p.66.

8   Theodore E. Zorn, 'Bosses and Buddies: Constructing and Performing Simultaneously Hierarchical and Close Friendship Relationships,' in Julia T. Wood and Steve Duck, *Under-studied Relationships* (California: Sage, 1995), p.140.

9   Michael Argyle, *op.cit.,* p.40.

CHAPTER NINE

SOUL MATES

The film *Sleepless in Seattle,* released in 1993, has left a small but perceptible dent in popular culture on both sides of the Atlantic. In case you've never seen it, the story begins with eight-year-old Jonah Baldwin calling a radio psychologist on Christmas Eve and making his father Sam tell the nation how lonely they've been since the death of Jonah's mother.

Across the country in Baltimore, Annie Reed listens to the syndicated programme with tears in her eyes. She's engaged to Walter – but Sam's words make her wonder if she's made the right choice.

For the rest of the film, Sam and Annie stumble in will-they-won't-they fashion towards their climactic first encounter, which occurs (where else) at the top of the Empire State Building in New York:

> *Jonah walks over to her. He puts his hand out. She shakes it solemnly.*
> JONAH: I'm Jonah. *(Nodding back to Sam)* That's my dad. His name is Sam.
> ANNIE: Hi, Jonah. Sam. *(Indicating Jonah's teddy bear)* And who is this?
> JONAH: Howard.
> ANNIE: Howard.
> *Sam nods. Smiling. Starting to put it all together. Annie smiles. Still nervous. No one knows what to do next. Just then, one of the elevator operators CLEARS HIS THROAT.*
> SAM: We'd better go.
> *Annie nods. Sam holds out his hand.*
> SAM: Shall we?

> *Annie slips her hand into his. It feels comfortable, natural,*
> *right.*
> ANNIE: *Sam?*
> *He looks at her.*
> ANNIE: *It's nice to meet you.*
> *Jonah makes a triumphant little double-fist gesture to him-*
> *self as the elevator doors close.*
> EXT. THE EMPIRE STATE BUILDING – NIGHT. WE SEE
> THE BUILDING *from above, all lit up, a romantic confec-*
> *tion, the world's largest Valentine.*
> *The CAMERA PULLS BACK and we see the United*
> *States spread out before us, with lights twinkling every-*
> *where. FADE OUT.*[1]

Like most romances, *Sleepless in Seattle* ends on a point of arrival. When Annie slips her hand into Sam's – a man she has never met – it feels 'comfortable, natural, *right*'. These two individuals are pieces of a pair. They were 'meant for' one another, and the movie shows us destiny bringing them together. That done – we are left to assume – all else is plain sailing. We heave an empathetic sigh. They live happily ever after.

We just *love* this stuff. Sam and Annie play out one of the abiding myths of our culture – the myth in which a man and a woman overcome every obstacle to discover perfect love. We cherish the myth, and we strive to make it real in our own experience.

Many of us broadcast our credentials just as Sam does in the movie – except with more forethought and calculation. 'Bubbly 41-year-old, loves theatre and riverside walks, seeks similar' is a sincere effort to pinpoint another individual whose personality might gel with yours and who is, at least, available enough to be browsing the personal columns.

And yet we're also aware that in romance we gamble on lengthening odds. The guy getting the girl is one thing; the guy setting up house with the girl is something else entirely. On the basis of social statistics, a *Sleepless in Seattle II* could well show Sam and Annie five years down the road, fighting like cats and dogs, and suing for divorce.[2]

WHY WE LOVE AND HATE MARRIAGE

Surveys suggest that marriages are still – marginally – more likely to survive than implode, and generally do better than less formalised arrangements like cohabitation.[3]

But the difficulty of the transition from singleness is almost proverbial. Hence the black humour of the marriage joke – a staple of stand-up comedy, and ritually invoked at weddings as a reminder of the groom's place in the gender war. To take examples at random:

Marriage is not a word. It is a sentence – a life sentence.

Marriage puts a ring on a woman's finger and two rings under the man's eyes.

Love is one long sweet dream, and marriage is the alarm clock.[4]

It's a credit to the power of love (or perhaps just a reminder of its anaesthetic effects) that against the backdrop of this grim folk wisdom men and women still want so urgently to pair off and live together.

On the whole, the stakes have been raised a good deal by our changing expectations. The psychological importance of the partner relationship has increased enormously in the last hundred years, more or less in proportion as its economic significance has declined.

A woman will less often rely on a man to meet all her financial needs, and a man will less often expect a woman to devote herself entirely to domestic management. And as they have grown in social equality and self-sufficiency, they have also started to expect far more of one another as sources of emotional, sexual and spiritual fulfilment.

The general pattern is one of high hopes, sometimes bitter disappointments, and a kickback that makes most of us think twice before we clothe our love in the boat-burning vows of a formal marriage ceremony. Hence the increasing popularity of living together as a kind of experimental half-way house.

And yet the case for long-term partnerships like marriage remains compelling. Research repeatedly shows that people in stable long-term relationships have better mental health, experience less stress, and can expect to live longer.[5] Similarly, the evidence for the benefits to children – in contrast to the emotional, psychological and educational risks of parental separation and divorce – is plain and overwhelming.[6] So what's the problem?

DECISION AND DESIRE

Love, as someone has observed, 'is much nicer to be in than an automobile accident, a tight girdle, a higher tax bracket, or a holding pattern over Philadelphia'.[7] That's a slight understatement. Going on between other people, love may appear absurd and incomprehensible. Fallen into yourself, it is probably the most wonderful gift life offers.

Love you fall into, though, is love of a very specific kind. It is *passionate* in three senses: it roots itself in the guts and not the mind; it is characterised by intense hunger and desire; and it lifts the lover into a state of almost religious ecstasy.

Being in love seems self-evidently 'natural, right'. Your whole being is seized by a virtually irresistible need to be with, to have, or to possess the beloved – which is why unrequited love can reduce you to such utter misery.

Passionate love is what we routinely see portrayed in popular movies and commercials. There's a reason for this. Passionate love burns brightest when the beloved is still unattained – just as physical hunger is most intense when there's no meal in the offing. Obstacles separating the lover from the beloved provide a classic source of dramatic tension and a strong basis for plot: boy meets girl, boy loses girl, boy and girl are united. In this way, the media both celebrates passionate romance and shapes our expectations of it.

The problem is what happens *next.* In dramatic terms, boy and girl getting together ties off the plot and brings the story to a tidy close. But real life doesn't stop there. It's characteristic of passion that, sooner or later, your very success in attaining the beloved will begin to soothe and subdue the hunger known as 'being in love'. The elation fades. You slowly descend to earth.

It's at this point that some may conclude, with Somerset Maugham, that love is 'a dirty trick played on us to achieve continuation of the species'.

More likely, though, and eased on with a little misunderstanding and friction, a new story will emerge. In this story, the first partner is no longer the yearned-for and unattained prize, but an obstacle preventing us from going through the cycle of passionate love again, with someone else. Someone who, we suppose, will match us and meet our needs more perfectly. Someone we were 'really' meant for.

Cue betrayal of intentions, emotional damage to third parties, a great deal of unhappiness, and the high probability that this second ride on the rollercoaster of passion will end in much the same place as the first.

Whether this situation is better, or worse, than being shackled into an unhappy marriage – and for whom – isn't a debate worth going into here. From a relational point of view, neither is satisfactory. But if long-term romantic relationships are worth having – and the evidence indicates overwhelmingly that they are – we might ask how they can be made to work. The answer, I think, begins with understanding what it means to love.

TAKING THE R OPTION IN FINDING YOUR SOUL MATE

At the end of the day, passion is not merely an experience. Romantic relationships in Western culture begin with a passionate conflagration – a whirlwind that picks you up and transports you. But as the relationship matures, passion ceases to be an outside force acting upon you and emerges as a *quality sustained and furthered by your own actions.*

When people say the passion has gone out of a relationship, almost always they mean that the spontaneous rush of love has evaporated and they now feel beached. But love isn't something you feel, or get; it is something you *do.*

A character in Louis de Bernières' novel *Captain Corelli's Mandolin* puts the point neatly:

> *Love is a temporary madness, it erupts like volcanoes and then subsides. And when it subsides you have to make a decision. You have to work out whether your roots have so entwined together that it is inconceivable that you should ever part. Because this is what love is. Love is not breathlessness, it is*

not excitement, it is not the promulgation of promises of eternal passion, it is not the desire to mate every second minute of the day, it is not lying awake at night imagining that he is kissing every cranny of your body. No, don't blush, I am telling you some truths. That is just being 'in love', which any fool can do. Love is what is left over after the being in love has burned away, and this is both an art and a fortunate accident.[8]

In all but its opening phases, a relationship does not tip passion out of the sky like rain. Once you're off the starting blocks, you *create* passion in the relationship, not by keeping your partner unattainable, but by deepening your mutual knowledge and appreciation and constantly constructing the relationship by putting the other's needs first.

Hard work? Yes – but we can almost guarantee that you won't increase the passion in your relationship any other way. And we mean 'increase' – not just 'save' or 'preserve'. Too often we get to a point where we think we know the other person, and even take a perverse pride in being able to predict his or her responses.

This is a presumption and a damaging mistake. Your partner is one of a kind; inexhaustible, irreplaceable, full of surprises, and the source of all the passion you will ever want – if you make the effort to get and stay close.

1. Know a soul mate when you see one

In the movie *Four Weddings and a Funeral*, one of the hapless bachelors shares these golden thoughts on courtship:

I always just hoped that I'd meet some nice friendly girl, like the look of her, hope the look of me didn't make her physically sick, then pop the question and, um, settle down and be happy. It worked for my parents. Well, apart from the divorce and all that.

There's some truth in the quip that getting married should be made more difficult. You don't improve long-term partnerships by handcuffing partners together; you do improve them by helping partners get along. And the first step along that road is picking the right partner. Because – with all due respect to the writers of *Sleepless in Seattle* – you really can't trust destiny to do the job for you.

The pool from which most of us select a partner is usually rather small. And the busier we are, the smaller it gets. It's not uncommon, therefore, to find twenty- and thirty-something professionals making decisions not about whether X is better than Y, but whether X is better than no one.

Pressures like these only increase the chances that you will jump first and ask questions later. So if you want to make any kind of realistic assessment of compatibility, one thing to look at is pacing yourself in getting close to someone. It's too important a decision to mess up.

The issue is not simply whether you like or fancy the person; it's whether your two lives can meld. The kinds of things you need to know up-front are:

- How far your goals correspond in key areas like career and child-raising.

- How many leisure interests and activities you can enjoy together.

- Whether either of you has a potentially deal-breaking commitment to, say, a professional vocation or a religious belief.

- How comfortable you feel around each other's friends and family.

It's finding enough overlap in these 'bonding areas' that lays the foundation for a workable relationship. Areas where you don't match will potentially be sources of conflict. And while conflict goes with the territory in any close relationship, it's worth assessing up-front to what degree you are just storing up grief by trying to accommodate too many conflict areas.

This could, of course, be construed as an excuse to ditch a relationship that's no longer satisfactory, on the grounds that it was a mistake from the beginning. But the seductiveness of this argument should make you wary.

True, sometimes a relationship is just an unmitigated disaster. Far more often, though, the power and the passion are still there, and the problem lies not in the engine but in the way you're turning the key. For that reason, and for the sake of the others who may depend on the relationship working, it's worth thinking hard before you cut and run.

Ironically, one of the reasons some romantic relationships fail may be the very conscientiousness with which the spouses/partners put their children first. Christopher Vincent, a couples' psychiatrist at the Tavistock Marital Studies Institute in London, warned recently of a danger 'that children will become emotionally handicapped by parents whose primary investment is in their children rather than each other'. In other words, you may do yourself *and* your children a favour by taking some quality time alone with your partner.

2. Take fidelity seriously

Conventional thinking about fidelity is a muddle. True, most people consider it reprehensible to 'cheat' on someone. But at the same time, they think being 'faithful' has a slightly dull and boring ring to it. Sleeping with the same person all your life shows a certain lack of initiative, like going on holiday every year to Blackpool. People who do it are a bit sheltered, out of touch, tweedy, naïve. Only one rung up, in fact, from being celibate.

But if long-term relationships matter, fidelity immediately becomes a live issue. And it's no good fudging it. Fidelity isn't a timid retreat from the passions of the real world. It's the key driver of passion. It's the essence and the quality-mark of your commitment to your partner; the absolute, exclusive, and public commitment of yourself to another human being, bar nothing. Not for as long as it suits you, or while the feelings last, or until you have a knock-down fight, but in perpetuity. Not as a casual promise uttered under the influence of infatuation, but as a clear-headed decision on the way you are going to manage your life.

Nothing freezes a relationship quicker than one partner's loss of confidence in the other – the suspicion, even the faintest thought, that he or she might not be playing straight. It kills spontaneity, because you can only open yourself to another person if that other person is doing the same with you. For deceiver and deceived alike, the magic of shared trust simply dissolves.

How far you give your relationship formal status by getting married is an important decision here. Marriage should perhaps be seen as statement rather than status. The status of being married, evoked by the term 'wedlock,' is that of an effortful undertaking not easy to undo – an emphasis that sits uneasily with our culture's instinct to keep options open. Marriage as a statement, on the other hand, emphasises the on-going decision-making of the partners. To have married a person is to signal – to everyone – your decision to build your life with that individual.

A few years ago, I (Michael) asked my wife to buy me a wedding ring. The tradition when we'd married had been for a ring to be worn only by the bride. Looking back it seemed to me not only that this had unhelpful overtones (the woman as chattel), but that a ring should make the same public statement for me as it did for her – that we are totally committed to one another.

3. Be clear about what you mean by sexual compatibility

Conventional wisdom takes a slightly unhelpful line on this, generally urging that, as with a used car, you're more likely to avoid disappointment if you test-drive your partner first.

No one disputes the aim of having great sex. The problem is how you get there – and stay there. Sexual compatibility should be no more than a readiness to abandon restraint and give your soul mate a truly satisfying and exciting sexual experience. If you redefine it as a performance test, the implied goal of which is gratification for *you,* then even five hours of steamy, non-stop sex will tell you remarkably little. Diagnostically, sex just isn't very informative. In fact, it can confuse matters by seeming to establish an intimacy for which the real foundations may be rather slim.

Everybody has to make a decision over how and when to express physical affection, and clear-headedness on the matter is a big ask. Given how important soul mate selection is, however, it may be worth considering how far social pressure to have sex serves the purpose of setting up a strong, long-term relationship.

It's not prissy to be assertive about your own values. And it's probably true that most of what you need to know about your partner's sexuality can be found out just by talking.

Imagine a relationship in which the partners do not share a common language, and you will begin to appreciate how vital verbal communication is to the process of self-disclosure and mutual discovery. Talking is – apart from anything else – deeply underestimated as a form of foreplay. It is also the medium in which your friendship will be played out. If you can't bring yourself to talk, that in itself may tell you a lot about the future for your sexual communication – and indeed about the viability of your whole relationship.

On wider compatibility issues, a number of psychometric approaches have been devised which can predict – with some accuracy – how likely it is that a given relationship will last. More importantly, they also provide feedback that helps partners improve the way they relate, by addressing issues like assertiveness, active listening skills, avoidance and dominance.[9]

4. Remember you need all kinds of relationships

We've suggested it's a key to the R option to make your partner relationship high-priority, close, exclusive, and passionate. This involves lifestyle choices. It's worth remembering, however, that close relationships can implode if the partners feel isolated.

When your relationship goes through a rough patch – and most do, sooner or later – it's helpful to have balanced your fidelity to your partner with the maintaining of other supportive relationships. A trusted friend or family member can provide a safe and discreet 'offloading point' when your main relationship isn't firing on all cylinders.

Close friends and family with whom you've maintained a relationship guarantee you somebody to talk things over with, the opportunity to get some perspective, the chance to consider alternative solutions, and a person who might be willing to act as mediator.

And don't forget – if you suddenly get left on your own, as happened to Sam and Jonah at the beginning of the movie, you'll want all the help you can get.

---

1   *Sleepless In Seattle*, by Jeff Arch. Rewritten by Nora Ephron & Delia Ephron, 10 May 1992.

2   Most people don't realise that this same jaundiced expectation is implicit in the term *honeymoon*. The OED quotes Blount (1656), who tells us the word is: 'applyed to those marryed persons that love well at first, and decline in affection afterwards; it is hony now, but it will change as the Moon.'

3   It's estimated that around 40% of marriages beginning now will end in divorce – in both the UK and the USA. The average length of a marriage in the UK is 9 years (7 years in the USA). On the face of it, this still compares favourably with the

survival rates of cohabitation (average 2–3 years). However, cohabitation increasingly functions as a form of pre-marriage, a transient state which either moves on to dissolution or to an upgrading of commitment. In the USA, for example, the percentage of marriages preceded by cohabitation rose from about 10 per cent for those marrying between 1965 and 1974 to over 50 per cent for those marrying between 1990 and 1994. See: Pamela J. Smock, 'Cohabitation in the United States: An Appraisal of Research Themes', *Annual Review of Sociology*, Volume 26 (August 2000).

4   With thanks to www.hitched.co.uk/jokes/index.asp

5   On these measurements, married people of both genders consistently do better than singles. Divorcees do worst of all – possibly because loss can be compounded by feelings of rejection and failure. Among the statistics: coronary heart disease kills 176 per thousand married men, 237 per thousand single men, and 362 per thousand divorced men. Divorced men are almost four times more likely to die in car accidents than married men, and divorced women three times more likely than married women. As to mental health, a classic and much replicated study showed that 41% of women *without* a strong supportive relationship suffered depression in response to a stressful life event. The figure for those *with* a strong supportive relationship was 10%. See J. J. Lynch, *The Broken Heart* (Basic Books, 1977); G. W. Brown & T. Harris, *Social Origins of Depression* (Tavistock, 1978); also Michael Argyle, 'The effects of relationships on wellbeing', in Nicola Baker, *Building a Relational Society* (Aldershot: Arena, 1996).

6   Interestingly, this is most readily perceived by women, almost 80% of whom in a recent *Prima* poll declared that marriage was vital for stable family life. The same proportion agreed that married couples should get tax breaks. (Quoted in Melanie Phillips, *Sunday Times,* 7 March 1999).

7   Attributed to Judith Viorst.

8   Louis de Bernières, *Captain Corelli's Mandolin* (London: Minerva, 1995), p.281.

9   See, for example, Blaine J. Fowers, Kelly H. Montel, & David H. Olson, 'Predicting Marital Success For Premarital Couple Types Based on PREPARE', *Journal of Marital & Family Therapy*, 1996, Vol.22, No.1, pp.103–119.

CHAPTER TEN

SEX

There's a classic TV clip of the former Poet Laureate, Sir John Betjeman. He's in his seventies, and a young interviewer is pushing him in his wheelchair up to the top of a hill.

At the crest, they pause to survey the poet's beloved English countryside. By and by, the interviewer looks earnest and asks, 'Sir John, looking back over your life, what is it you most regret?'

Rug over his knees, Betjeman furrows his brow and replies crisply: 'I regret that I didn't get enough sex.'

WHY SEX IS NOT OFTEN ALL THAT IT COULD BE

Not getting enough sex isn't only a complaint of poets laureate. Many of our difficulties with sex stem, we think, from the way society trains us to think of sexuality.

For example, we seldom ask what sex is 'for'. Of course, it has the crucial role of conceiving children – but this is not what occupies most people's minds when they get into bed with each other. The common view is that sex doesn't have a purpose. Sex is simply fun for its own sake, like going to the movies, playing volleyball, or eating ice cream.

This tends to be held as true irrespective of the kind of relationship you have with your sexual partner. If the two of you are madly in love, you probably won't pause to analyse what part sex plays in your relationship – you will just get on with it. And for a couple who met two hours previously at a club, the chances are neither of them are thinking beyond breakfast the next morning anyway. In either situation, if you're lucky, sex works its fairground-ride magic immediately – then lets you out of the gate.

Ironically, though, the idea that sex has no function but to provide instant, glorious, and irresistible pleasure is dangerous – because in the end it prevents both partners from having truly and lastingly great sex.

For one thing, sex-as-recreation increasingly turns it into sex-as-sport, into something *you have to be good at.*

No accomplished tennis player wants to spend two hours on court with a rank amateur. Likewise, in sex, a fear may persist that you will lose the respect of your partner, either by failing to turn in an Olympic performance or, worse, just by having breasts the wrong size or forgetting to brush your teeth.

Second, in the nitty-gritty real world, being in bed with someone isn't *automatically* a turn-on. Even the blinding ecstasy of first-time sex won't guarantee that both partners have their expectations met and their desires fulfilled.

In that sense, sex is as much a careful, co-operative exercise as moving a piano up a staircase. If one person lets go, the other one's in trouble. This is true at all sorts of levels. In the workplace it's the point where flirting turns into harassment; in lovemaking it's the point where the less assertive partner – often the woman – begins to feel used.

Third, and closely related to the above, there is the problem of *men.*

We don't think it's stereotyping our gender to say that men aren't that terrific at the huggy-cuddly side of sex. They doze off soon after orgasm. They revert depressingly fast to a preoccupation with share dealing, football, beer and cars. They find it an enormous effort to listen without interjecting 'Well, there's a simple answer to that one...'

In short, men often don't understand women. Equally, no doubt, women don't understand men. And probably the complaint that 'my partner doesn't understand me' underlies millions of relationships in which sex has lapsed and – often as a consequence – the partners are drifting towards separation.

THE PURPOSE OF SEX IS RELATIONSHIP

Recently, the head of the counselling team at Cambridge University was telling me (Michael) about relationships around the colleges. He passed on this remark from an undergraduate: 'The issue now for students is not where we can get sex, but where we can find *commitment.'*

The significance of the 'C' word should not be underestimated. The idea that romantic relationships should be 'forever' is not, in fact, a conspiracy by the world's main religions, nor the invention of the pro-family lobby. Anyone lucky enough to have fallen in love will tell you that desire for permanence flows from sexual desire like water from a spring. Every year, countless lovers vow eternal faithfulness to each other – and sincerely mean it.

Given that up to half of them are projected to suffer a separation – and sometimes two or three separations – their confidence and belief are staggering. Whatever the track record, and notwithstanding the caution displayed over taking vows in marriage, people seem unable to let go of the idea that love is, in some sense, 'eternal'.

The problem, of course, is that love, like a goldfish, thrives and grows only if we feed it. Taking the R option in intimate relationships means – in summary – choosing wisely and sticking by your choice. That makes sense because long-term, stable relationships are good for you, good for your partner, good for social support, and good for children if you ever have any. But the R option also means watching over that relationship and making it flourish. And in this, sex has a pivotal role.

Television documentaries on marriage occasionally feature couples who have chosen not to have sex until their wedding day. To most viewers this choice will seem precious, over-scrupulous, even bizarre. If no one else is hurt by it, what earthly reason is there for *not* having sex?

In many cases, the reason is religious. But there is also a relational logic behind it, and the logic has to do with recognising that sex does, after all, have a purpose – whether you attend church or not. It is an exclusive intimacy on which the one, central and critical relationship of your life is founded. It is a locked vault to which only you and your partner have the key.

Naturally, there is nothing to prevent you taking Cole Porter's line that 'even educated fleas do it,' and so you may as well get on and do it too, with any consenting third party. But that is to miss the whole point. The R option with sex is to deliberately conduct yourself sexually in a way that deepens your relationship with your partner. By design, you do not make yourself available in this way to just anyone. But in the one relationship that really matters, involving a public declaration of life-long commitment, you give yourself completely and without reservation.

Of course, you remain a sexual being outside as well as inside that relationship, just as a tennis player remains a tennis player even when he or she is not playing tennis. But as another song says, the governing principle for all other potential sexual encounters is: 'My body says let's go; my heart says no.'[1] This isn't prudery or emasculation. It's clear-headed self-management.

'Le mariage,' wrote Casanova, 'c'est le tombeau de l'amour' ('marriage is the tomb of love'). If that is true, the fault lies not in the principle of the long-term relationship, but in the way the partners involved oversee it.

Partnerships today are subject to more – and more intense – pressures than ever before. The demands of work. The demands of children. The demands of travel. But if two people can ground their commitment to one another in mutual and unrestrained sexual passion, it won't be easy to separate them on anything else.

TAKING THE R OPTION IN SEX

It's not hard to find advice on sexual technique. Technique, though, really has very little to do with whether sex is fulfilling. Consequently, taking the R option in sex will involve, among other things, figuring out what kind of wider relationship will make sexuality flourish. If you want a good crop of tomatoes, you'd better get out there with the watering can.

The following points lay out a general direction and approach.

1. See sex as something individual to your partner

If you value your relationship with your partner, it's pointless treating sex as a skill in which he or she excels or is deficient. There is, in that sense, no such thing as being abstractly good or bad in bed. You cannot think of another person as being a car in need of a new clutch, or a school listed in national performance league tables.

Your partner's sexuality is embedded in the person he or she is; it is unique and individual to him or her in the same way as the *Mona Lisa* is unique and individual in art, or the landscape of the Western Highlands of Scotland is unique and individual in topography. That person *is* your sexuality. You cultivate shared sexual passion privately and exclusively with that person and without reference to any external benchmark of 'performance'.

Of course, in a culture where sex is so much 'in your face' – on the street, in the media, via the Internet – you're under constant pressure to make comparisons. Indeed, with commercial pornography, feeding dissatisfaction is the name of the marketing game.

But you cannot play that game without immediately reducing your partner to a commodity – a supplier of sexual kicks you might obtain in greater quantities, or on better terms, from someone else. And the further you go down that road, the less you are likely to invest in your own relationship, and the more your sexuality will become unstitched.

2. Be partner-centred

To focus on the relationship in sex comes down to focusing on your partner's needs and desires – which, of course, may be quite different from your own.

A helpful literature has emerged recently highlighting the broad differences in the way men and women relate.[2] If it's ever occurred to you to ask why you like to jog a gentle 5,000 metres in sex while your partner prefers the 100-metre dash – this information may be useful to you.

But there are also matters of individual taste, of what your partner individually likes or dislikes, and you will only find that out by spending time and listening. Also, it's worth watching simple things like politeness. There's a lot of difference relationally between saying 'I really want you but I'm just too tired' and saying 'Push off, I'm trying to sleep'.

3. Increase the breadth of your relationship

Sex has a better chance of staying exciting if you mix it with a wider portfolio of activities. Granted this isn't always easy to accomplish with busy careers and children. Nevertheless – all other things being equal – it's likely that two partners will remain interesting to each other sexually if they remain interesting to each other as people. It's from life shared in the round, and not from sex on its own, that qualities like trust, friendship, sensitivity and mutual understanding arise.

If you do nothing much together except share a bedroom, two things are likely to happen. First, you will gradually narrow your appreciation of your partner until he or she is little more than a supplier of sexual services – not something calculated to keep the spark of passion alive. And second, if the sex goes wrong (as it probably will in these circumstances), there won't be much else left in the relationship to sustain it.

4. Set your limits outside the relationship

Being able to preserve and enhance your relationship with your partner depends a lot on the way you act when you're apart. Do you value your relationship? Then it's worth examining how you can avoid triggering competing claims on your intimacy.

Somewhere in the complexities of modern gender etiquette there is a point where gentle banter with another person will be taken as an explicit come-on – whether you mean it that way or not.

One of the choices you may want to make concerns where to set boundaries. Situations you won't put yourself in. Advances you won't tolerate. Subjects you won't talk about. Ways in which you signal – discreetly but clearly – that you are not available and not to be messed with. If you decide in advance what you will and will not do, and stand by that commitment, you remain in control.

5. Make sex the garden to which only you and your partner have the key

In the R option, sex belongs to you and your partner. It is your secret, your joint property. Nobody else has a right to know about it or to claim a part in it. And your readiness to defend this privacy is part of what gives your shared sexual life its fire.[3] Even a helping professional, counselling you on difficulties you may experience with sex, doesn't enter the relationship.

It may be worth thinking through, therefore, how the relationship will be affected by advances from people outside. Much interaction between men and women has a low-voltage current passing through it. How you react to this – whether it flatters you, whether you rise to it or instigate it, whether you reserve to yourself the right to flirt with other people – may have consequences for the health of your relationship with your partner.

If you enjoy the sexual flattery of others, you are giving part of your sexuality away and establishing conditions that can undermine your partner's confidence in you. If, on the other hand, you communicate to your partner, 'I want you to know that I have no room in my life for anyone but you',[4] this powerfully reinforces the bond between you. Fidelity can be a serious turn-on.

6. Pace yourselves

In his book *Kosher Sex,* Rabbi Schmuley Boteach offers this diagnosis of sexual dysfunction:

> *Too many couples try to make their marriages proceed along a straight line. They share a bed constantly, and wonder why their sex life loses its spark after a short while. They have sex several times a week, with no break, and wonder why it comes in short, forgettable spasms.*[5]

Three millennia ago, he points out, Judaism devised an ingenious solution to this. For two weeks in every month, marriage partners are encouraged to indulge their sexual passions to the limit. Then, as the woman's menstrual cycle begins – and 'just before monotony sets in' – they enter a matching two-week period of strict sexual abstinence. During this time, they have a chance to develop the intellectual and emotional side of their relationship. They also build up an intense sexual hunger, which then drives and sustains them for another two weeks of indulgence. And so the cycle goes on.

How exactly this applies outside the disciplines of Judaistic faith isn't clear. But the principle embodies some practical good sense. As Boteach rightly observes, men in particular 'have a very short sexual attention span, and quickly tire of an available body that provides no adventure and can be conquered without a chase'.

'Two weeks on, two weeks off' may not appeal to everyone as a sexual regime. But if sex is losing its edge for you both, why not pump up the passion a little by deliberately and consensually putting physical contact off-limits for an agreed length of time? Maybe it's not as crazy as it sounds.

7 Prioritise intimacy in your lifestyle

In a long-term partnership, sex is important. It's not icing on the cake. It's a fundamental element – arguably *the* fundamental element – of the relationship. You should not willingly allow it to be crowded by fatigue, overwork or anxiety, or under pressure of children.

Schedule it, just like any other priority. If you both want sex, you both need to fit it into your diaries. Use a little ingenuity. Children may be glad to visit grandparents and get rid of you for a night. With forethought, days off work can be made to coincide. If you're a night person, and your partner is a morning person, find an excuse to miss lunch together.

It's just plain unrealistic that sex needs to be spontaneous. Going to the theatre isn't any more fun just because you buy the tickets five minutes before the curtain goes up. Plan sex in advance and enjoy the pleasures of travelling hopefully *and* arriving.

---

1   Christina Aguilera, *Genie in a Bottle*. Written by David Frank, Steve Kipner and Pam Sheyne. Produced by David Frank and Steve Kipner.

2   See, for example: Deborah Tannen, *You Just Don't Understand* (London: Virago, 1991).

3   An exception to this is a situation where you need advice from a trusted friend or professional. Even in these cases, however, you should exercise care over your choice of confidante and the nature of the information you disclose. Nobody will take better care of your secrets than you do.

4   Or, if your relationship is such that you know you can absolutely depend on each other's loyalty.

5   Schmuley Boteach, *Kosher Sex: A Recipe for Passion and Intimacy* (London: Hodder & Stoughton, 1999), p.73.

CHAPTER ELEVEN

LOSS

I look up at the night sky. Is anything more certain than that in all those vast times and spaces, if I were allowed to search them, I should nowhere find her face, her voice, her touch? She died. She is dead. Is the word so difficult to learn?[1]

You *are* going to die. That is the one event in your future you can predict with absolute certainty. And probably, by the time you get there, you will have endured the death of someone close to you – parent, sibling, partner, close friend, even a child.

We all know this. And, for as long as we can, we try to ignore it. Popular culture colludes in this – you won't, for instance, see a funeral parlour in your local shopping centre, offering real oak coffins at a discount. For most of the time, the very old – the almost-dead – are kept discreetly out of view. And once death has taken place, the remains are removed by professional services as though they were radioactive waste.

Not surprisingly, our collective inability to deal with death affects even those who see it most often. Staff in accident and emergency units, so skilled in preserving life, feel inadequately trained to cope with death, grief, and bereavement. The job of informing next of kin is one that most doctors dread. Saving life, and coping with life being lost, are fundamentally different things.

BOARDING THE TRAIN

From the viewpoint of relationships, there are two things worth noting about the experience of dying.

First, a good way of keeping your *body* alive is to keep your *relationships* alive. Study after study has highlighted the correlation between good health and sociality. Research conducted recently in Norway shows that increased risk of dying is associated not just with a lack of supportive relationships, but with a loss of social participation and of a sense of control.[2] In other words, the worst thing you can do is be a recluse. Hermits die sooner.

Instinctively realising this, many older people go out of their way to stay fit, vigorous, and socially involved. But meaningful interaction relies on some expectation of a tomorrow, on there being time ahead to fill with plans, hopes, appointments, projects, goals. Take that time away, and – according to disengagement theory – those life-giving relationships may be cashed in.

The second thing to note is that, even if you carry your close relationships to your deathbed, you cannot take them with you. Yes, it's hackneyed – but death really is like a departure. You leave others behind. You step onto the carriage, a lone passenger, and the train draws you away towards whatever lies on the other side.

At that moment, all your relationships – remote or intimate, bad or good – simultaneously end. Fall under a bus, of course, and they'll end in mid-flow, like a book with the final pages torn away. But most of us don't fall under buses. We see death coming. And we have time, if we want, to tie up the loose ends before we go.

WAVING FROM THE PLATFORM

Relationships also lie at the heart of bereavement – of being left on the platform as the train pulls away.

The word 'bereavement' is derived from the Anglo-Saxon *beriafien,* meaning 'to be robbed'. In close relationships, bereavement may seem less like a departure than a mugging. It assaults you, snatches something away from you, leaves you bleeding. Just as you need time to recover from physical trauma, so you need time to recover from relationship loss. It's a healing process. You don't have much choice but to let the programme run.

It helps, of course, if there are other people on the platform with you. But the number of people able to share in grief may be small, and the dynamics between them may be complicated by other factors. A woman whose partner has died will share her grief with the children, but, if the children are young, may also have to cope with the behavioural fallout resulting from their loss of a father.

Around that circle of front-line grieving, there can be something of a ring of fire. C. S. Lewis comments in the wake of his wife's death:

> *An odd by-product of my loss is that I'm an embarrassment to everyone I meet. At work, at the club, in the street, I see people, as they approach me, trying to make up their minds whether they'll 'say something about it'. I hate it if they do, and if they don't.*[3]

Things could be worse. In the Makao District of nineteenth-century New Guinea, a widower lost all civil rights and became a social outcast, unable to cultivate a garden, appear in public, cross the village, or hunt in daylight.[4] But the psychology of fear behind such customs isn't so very different in the modern West. As Lewis notes, 'Whenever I meet a happily married pair, I can feel them thinking, "One or other of us must some day be as he is now."'[5]

There's a sense, of course, in which a dead person remains present, partly because all the mental apparatus you've developed to conduct the relationship can't be 'uninstalled'.

I (David) remember a sepia portrait of a boy that hung in my grandmother's living room. He was my mother's brother – my only uncle – who died of tuberculosis when he was six. I can't imagine him as an adult – he's stuck forever in childhood. So far as I recall, my grandmother never spoke of him, but the experience of lost children being trapped in a parent's memory is a common one. And the longer grief drags on, the more mannered the memory becomes. A dead person cannot generate new dialogue or new experience. The script is already complete. He or she can no longer surprise.[6]

Where the dead *do* surprise in Anthony Minghella's film *Truly Madly Deeply,* rematerialising with all their endearing flaws, the point seems to be that, if bereavement is to succeed as a healing process, the dead must be allowed to leave.

If you wish, you can tend the space in your heart as a sort of sacred shrine. But you can *fill* it only with other, active relationships.

TAKING THE R OPTION WHEN FACED WITH LOSS

An awareness of relationships doesn't necessarily draw the sting out from bereavement or steel your resolve in the face of death. But the R option does offer ways of managing these massive relational events – for yourself and for those you love.

Not least, it stresses the need to bring dying back into the realm of ordinary human experience. Being told you have six months to live doesn't turn you into a leper. Nor does losing your partner or child. At these moments, isolation is the last thing you need. If ever relationships matter, they matter here.

1. Be a person first

One thing worth working through is how dying affects your identity. If you discover tomorrow morning that you have an inoperable cancer, you don't suddenly become 'a cancer patient', or 'somebody who's dying'. You are you – controlling this last phase of your life as you've controlled all the others. At some earlier point you might have chosen to sacrifice your life to protect your loved ones. As things stand, you have taken this road, and reached this place. Current misfortune only turns you into an object of pity if you give it that permission.

Becoming pitiable is a state in a relationship that upsets things on both sides. That's why people who are dying sometimes find it easier to talk to others who are in the same condition, finding 'friends for dying' while they stay in a hospice or nursing home. Remaining yourself – and recognising the selfhood of a dying person you're visiting – plays an important part in keeping the relationship viable.

2. Complete relationships before you leave

Have you ever heard of anyone wishing on his deathbed that he'd spent more time at the office? In the final stage of life, most of us want to focus on relationships, and particularly on relationships with those dear to us.

All important relationships need a 'settling of accounts'. People need to say goodbye, clear up misunderstandings, articulate 'important things', make provision for the young and the weak. If this doesn't happen, the dying person departs with a sense of unfinished business, and those left behind can be lumbered with a guilt they no longer have the means to resolve.

At a merely practical level, death also closes a window of opportunity. You'll never again be able to ask this person for an opinion, or draw on his or her unique fund of information about your family's history. Not, of course, that such things need to be left to the last minute.

I (David) remember sitting on a park bench with my father at the age of about twenty-five, and telling him I thought he'd done a good job of bringing me up. Looking back, it was a slightly back-handed compliment. But it marked a point of completion. And the longer I live, the more thankful I am that I made a point of saying it.

3. Stay connected

The difficulties surrounding death – the sense of being on your own, the need for practical assistance during illness, the terrible feelings of loss if you're left behind – can all be handled more successfully if you have strong supportive relationships.

Some communities generate these more readily than others. Muslims and Jews, for example, each tend to share geographic location, as well as institutions like schools and places of worship that draw members into regular contact. Extended families also are strong, with the result that any one individual is likely to have numerous relatives on hand to help in time of need.

Mainstream liberal society in the UK and the USA lacks this community tradition. Consequently, there will be fewer people near the middle of the radar diagram (see Figure 1), and a concomitantly greater loss, as well as fewer friends to fall back on, if one of them is removed.

As we argue in the chapter on rootedness, building a base of relationships, or making contributions to a 'relational pension', requires long-term commitment and effort. Yet it's precisely in the context of coping with death and bereavement that such effort pays dividends – all round. How well you handle such challenges ahead depends very much on the way you build and prioritise your relationships now.

4. Talk about it

Communication eases the grief reaction. A recent study of bereaved parents showed that the couples who communicated over their loss processed their grief more quickly and reported higher degrees of marital satisfaction later on.[7]

Similarly with communication during the dying process. How a dying person handles relationships during this traumatic period will have consequences long afterwards. Permitting and appreciating someone's help may save that person later from the burden of feeling they didn't do enough.

As one carer has said, 'I think that's why I feel relatively contented now, because nobody could have possibly done more for a man than I did for him.'[8]

5. Be there with practical help even if you can't 'make things better'

In some cases, the best thing you can do for a dying or bereaved person is not to make a big deal out of showing sympathy, but simply to be there for the practical things.

It usually only adds to the awkwardness if the person feels that he or she is suddenly being handled like a piece of expensive glassware. Friends, for example, can help those who grieve by caring for boisterous young members of the family when the parents need some quiet and privacy.

6. Take religion seriously

Bad things happen to good people, and for no discernible reason. C. S. Lewis, for twenty years a stout defender of Anglican Christianity, found himself asking:

> *Meanwhile, where is God? This is one of the most disquieting symptoms. When you are happy, so happy that you have no sense of needing Him, so happy that you are tempted to feel His claims upon you as an interruption, if you remember yourself and turn to Him with gratitude and praise, you will be – or so it feels – welcomed with open arms. But go to Him when your need is desperate, when all other help is vain, and what do you find? A door slammed in your face.*[9]

There is, at least, nothing glib in this. The misery of loss tends to bring us back to basics – and, inevitably, this is where belief in God suddenly becomes an issue.

Christian apologist though he was, C. S. Lewis nevertheless had to work through this own individual grief. The evidence that he did is poignantly recorded in a later part of the same book where he writes:

> *I have gradually been coming to feel that the door is no longer slammed and bolted. Was it my own frantic need that slammed it in my face?...On the other hand, 'Knock and it shall be opened.' But does knocking mean hammering and kicking the door like a maniac? And there's also, 'To him that hath shall be given.' After all, you must have a capacity to receive, or even omnipotence can't give.*[10]

Despite all the talk about religious belief being a crutch, few faiths offer much in the way of immediate help in suffering. Clearly there's not much to be gained by adopting this or that religion just as a kind of security blanket.

On the other hand – and this Lewis would doubtless affirm – certain understandings of God do have the power of putting death in context. Thomas More wrote in one of his letters that he longed to give up the Chancellorship of England and retire, not to play golf, but to contemplate the afterlife.

Searching out religious belief, to the point where you sense that you have both a ticket and a destination, will make boarding that final train very much less daunting.

---

1   C. S. Lewis, *A Grief Observed* (London, Faber & Faber, 1961) p.16. Lewis, an Oxbridge academic, was married – all too briefly – to the American novelist Joy Davidson. For sheer clarity and honesty, we have not found any better treatment of loss than this short book.

2   Odd Steffan Dalgard and Lise Lund Haheim, 'Psychosocial risk factors and mortality: A prospective study with special focus on social support, social participation, and locus of control in Norway' in *Journal of Epidemiology and Community Health*, 1998, Vol.52(8): 476–481.

3   C. S. Lewis, *op.cit.*, p.10.

4   See Dewi Rees, *Death and Bereavement – The psychological, religious and cultural interfaces* (London, Whurr Publishers Ltd, 1997) p.104.

5 C. S. Lewis, *op.cit.*, p.13.
6 The exception – occasionally – being at the reading of the will.
7 Sherrie Kamm, 'Psychological adjustment, relationship satisfaction, and communication in bereaved parents' (Dissertation Abstracts International: Section B: The
   Sciences and Engineering), 2000 Feb: Vol 60(7–8): 3568.
8 G. Howarth, 'Ageing and Society' in *Journal, 1998 (Abstract)*, Vol. 18 (6), p.684.
9 C. S. Lewis, *op.cit.*, p.9.
10 C. S. Lewis, *op. cit.*, p.38.

CHAPTER TWELVE

FORGIVENESS

Imagine everyone in Northern Ireland waking up with amnesia. People wouldn't be able to recall if they were Loyalists or Republicans. They wouldn't know about the Troubles, or have any old scores to settle. Overnight, the enmities dividing the Province would – quite literally – have been forgotten.

No doubt a society of amnesiacs would have other problems to contend with. Not least the fact that loving relationships are also dependent on memory. But the absurdity of the idea of cutting ourselves off from the past only shows how big a part memory plays in conflict – both political and personal.

'Forgive and forget', the proverb says blithely. But the whole problem with the past is that you *can't* forget as an act of will. The wrong done to you yesterday – by your boss, by your partner, by your friend, or by a whole class of people like 'the Catholics' or 'the Serbs' – has changed you forever. It is an event in your life story. And its psychological or material impact may be apparent for years ahead.

When these crises crop up – and sooner or later they will, in almost any relationship – you have only three alternatives.

- You can live with conflict (the bad marriage, the worker enduring a tyrannical boss, the cold war).

- You can pull out (divorce, resignation, ethnic cleansing).

- Or you can set out on the road to reconciliation.

Take the third option, though, and it won't be long before you are faced head-on with the issue of forgiveness.

WHY IT MATTERS IF WE DON'T FORGIVE

On 22 June 2001, the High Court in the UK made a ruling that, in effect, brought forward the release of the two boys who murdered the Liverpool toddler Jamie Bulger in 1993 – a watershed case that sent shock waves through the UK.

In the main, media pundits have condemned the criminal justice system for what many view as excessive leniency towards the culprits. Jamie Bulger's mother made this comment: 'Even though they are evil, I have to accept the killers will be released one day, but they should serve nothing less than fifteen years.'[1]

It's true, of course, that the death of Jamie Bulger is different from, say, a case of domestic violence. There is no pre-existing relationship here to be healed. The damage came out of the blue, from the action of complete strangers. Also, it had a scattergun effect, simultaneously affecting not just the child, but all those who loved and cared for him – including, by a process of empathy, a large part of the general public.

In the reaction it's provoked, though, this apparently motiveless killing is less distinctive. Here, as elsewhere, and quite understandably, the victims think first of retribution. An eye for an eye, and a tooth for a tooth. Mess me around, and I'll mess you around – and see if *you* like it.

To rush in with advice to forgive in these situations inevitably comes across as pious and insensitive. Forgiving may be a virtue, but only a fool would expect you to do it as a matter of routine. Almost by definition, we see forgiving wrongdoers – and especially serious wrongdoers – as lying some considerable distance beyond the call of duty. There's also a sense in which not forgiving is integral to justice. The lasting determination to remember war crimes, for example, has been instrumental in the success of trials, even fifty years after the crimes occurred.

To the extent that a wrong is an assault on the moral order, then, we should demand that justice is done. But to the extent that a wrong is an assault on a *relationship*, it may pay us to see the best outcome as lying in another direction – not in retribution, but in healing and reconciliation.

I mean 'pay' in a purely self-interested sense. You'll put up with a lot of stick from another person if you care for him or her and wish the relationship to continue. You can be hurt quite badly, yet still want to put things right.

But also, deciding *not* to forgive exacts its own cost. If your boss gives you a public tongue-lashing, you'll suffer a certain amount of direct damage to your ego. But you'll sustain a lot more damage if you nurse a grudge.

Bitterness may feel like the next best thing to vengeance, but you might as well have a migraine for all the damage it's going to do to its intended target. Studies repeatedly underline the link between repressed anger and alcoholism, ill-health, and sometimes fatal stress on other relationships.

Place this sort of social pathology in the context of a business or public service, and there are compelling reasons to take forgiveness seriously. Organisationally, you don't need many people who can't or won't forgive each other – in the sense of properly resolving past wrongs – before you have a serious problem on your hands. Resentful employees underperform, spread dissatisfaction, and may deliberately sabotage operations. There are simply too many sensitive relationships in an organisation, and too much at stake in terms of company profitability and quality of service, to risk this kind of damage to the relational architecture.

As for international politics, events in Kosovo, Northern Ireland, South Africa, Rwanda and the Middle East have brought the issue of forgiveness abruptly onto the negotiating table. According to the political commentator Donald W. Shriver Jr:

> If the conflict-ridden and conflict-prone peoples of the earth are to move away from a Hobbesian 'war of all against all' into forms of politics that are not merely war by other means, we must do something about the memories and the continuing legacies of the harms we have inflicted on each other in the recent or remote past ... A major 'something' that we have to enact is a social, political form of forgiveness.[2]

TAKING THE R OPTION WITH FORGIVENESS

Clearly, forgiveness isn't for the faint-hearted. Nor is it a simple, self-contained, or one-off event. You make a decision to forgive as part of the process of rebuilding a relationship. It's pulling the rip-cord on a plummeting connection. And it's a step that needs total commitment.[3]

Between communities, particularly, reconciliation involves a lengthy reconstruction of trust, and may begin with some pretty modest steps – for instance, the establishing of political structures that allow former enemies to co-exist in relative peace. At both the individual and community levels, however, some important principles apply.

1. Value the future more than the past

Broken relationships have their skirts caught in the doors of history. It seems incredible that a Serb could kill a Muslim to avenge a battle fought in 1389. But the action is unusual only in degree, not in kind. The Battle of the Boyne, the Reformation, the Crusades – memories of all these conflicts are being kept alive by one or another group in the world today. Often the events are merely backmarkers for a whole string of later exchanges that have entrenched animosity and perpetuated struggle.

That the past must be left behind for the sake of the future is a sentiment often expressed in the context of political peacemaking. But it's a serious and essential precondition. So long as one side is mentally revisiting the past for the purpose of apportioning blame, no real forgiveness is going to occur.

This applies just as powerfully in the personal realm. At some point, you have to let the past go – which means you have to stop yourself compiling a mental dossier against a person who's hurt you. It's not easy; you may have to remind yourself every day that you've decided to close this particular book. But it's only by adopting this kind of inner strength – a strength that says 'I'm big enough to stand above this' – that you'll free yourself from bitterness and self-pity.

Forgiveness is not the same as reconciliation. Forgiving is a unilateral act; reconciliation takes two. But the willingness to forgive – to stop telling the story of your grievance over and over again, to yourself and others – must be present before reconciliation can happen.

2. Assess honestly the depth of the wrong

Relationships can't be rescued without the consent – and usually the wholehearted commitment – of both parties.

Two Dutch sisters thrown into a Nazi labour camp for protecting Jews were viciously treated by one particular guard, as a result of which the older one died. Years later, the younger sister was invited to address a church meeting and saw this same guard in the congregation. Believing it a religious duty to forgive, she mustered the courage to confront him, and was shocked to find that conversion had removed any sense of personal responsibility for his former crimes.

Reconciliation demands contrition. In other words, the wrong must be named and acknowledged on both sides, in all its unpleasantness. If the person who committed the wrong refuses to take it seriously, or refuses to accept responsibility, or, for that matter, simply can't be found, then forgiveness cannot fulfil its function of healing the relationship. That doesn't mean it doesn't have value. But its benefits will be felt mainly in the mind of the person who's been wronged.

Of course, the problem can equally well lie on the side of the person doing the forgiving.

One orphaned refugee recalls the childless couple who took him in and adopted him. When he arrived at their house, they burned all of his old torn clothing except for one item – his shoes. These his father placed on the mantel as a reminder of what they'd rescued him from. In time, they became a tool of moral blackmail. The boy would never be allowed to forget his origins:

> *When I disappointed him in some way, he would walk to the mantel and pick up the shoes ... By the time I was a teenager, he didn't need to haul them down to remind me how much he and my mother had done for me; a glance was enough.*[4]

This method of exacting obedience, by harking back to the debt one person owes to another, isn't uncommon. Another method is to magnify the seriousness of the offence. Parents have been known to meet quite trifling offences with threats ranging all the way from 'Father Christmas won't come', to 'the police will arrest you', and 'God will send you to hell'.

Exaggerating the offence in this way is designed to provoke contrition and boost the share price of forgiveness. But in the long run, the effect is almost always further to undermine the relationship, not to repair it. As the refugee commented, 'By the time I was able to put my predicament into words, I no longer felt grateful at all.'

You can also understate the wrong being done to you. In a significant number of cases, forgiveness is made meaningless because the person on the receiving end of cruelty or abuse won't admit how despicably they've been treated.

There are various reasons for this. Young victims of child abuse, for example, may fear reprisals, or simply feel too ashamed to acknowledge what's gone on. Many more of us are guilty of overlooking bullying, advantage-taking and rudeness in order to avoid 'causing a scene'. We tell ourselves we're forgiving another person's conduct, when what we're really doing is practising denial and avoidance – reclassifying the incident as inconsequential.

3. Understand your role in the relationship breakdown

You can't ask someone who's committed a wrong against you to engage in deep self-examination – unless you're willing to reciprocate.

David Augsburger tells the story of a counsellor who'd slept with two of his clients. Finally he was discovered, and had to confess to his wife. He miserably – and sincerely – pleaded for her forgiveness, but she refused to give it. Not, though, for the reason you'd think. She told him:

> No, I will not forgive you. I do not want the kind of relationship with you in which you are the offender and I am the forgiver. I don't want you grateful and indebted to me for the rest of our lives. I want us to work through this until we both understand our parts in the problem, until we can accept each other ... You did the active part. I did the passive part in helping create a relationship that was open to outside invitations. Let's work it out until we're back together.[5]

Perhaps not all such breakdowns can be salvaged. But with those that can, the importance of preserving the basic parity of those involved is clearly important. Refuse to do this, and sooner or later the offender will tire of his or her role as debtor in the relationship, and further breakdown will ensue.

This is not to say that responsibility for every crisis in a relationship can be split pretty much down the middle. Sometimes one party will behave abysmally with no obvious provocation from the other. But however unjustly you feel you've been treated, you cannot avoid the fact that you, too, have weaknesses and breaking-points. Being wronged does not make you irreproachable. As the proverb says, it takes two to tango.

The same applies – though, admittedly, in a rather more complex way – to relationships between communities and nations.

Fifty years after the end of the Second World War, Japan and the USA are full allies and trading partners. Yet significant numbers of people in both nations still struggle with the horrors of the Pacific War. That war was topped and tailed by two of history's most devastating military actions – the surprise attack on Pearl Harbor in Hawaii, and the dropping of two atomic bombs on Hiroshima and Nagasaki.[6]

Like their counterparts in Britain, many ex-service personnel in the USA have demanded an apology from later Japanese governments for Japan's conduct during the war.[7]

It's less often recalled that while Japan was already suing for peace, the US General Henry H. Arnold pressed for 'as big a finale as possible'. On August 14 he bombed the now devastated Tokyo with a force of 828 B-29 bombers. Not a single plane was lost, and Japan's surrender was announced before most of them had returned to base.

Against that background, Donald Shriver tells the following story:

> *Tomohiko Teramoto, age twenty-eight, was making new connections between both sides of the debate when in the week of the fiftieth anniversary [of the outbreak of war] he decided to visit Pearl Harbor, a brave thing for a Japanese tourist to do in that particular week. He came, he said, because he had no direct experience of war, but he knew that 'it's bad to forget. Japanese should remember Pearl Harbor, and Americans should remember Hiroshima.'* [8]

The moral: be mindful of your own mistakes – not just the other person's.

It's a tough trick to pull. In the same year, John J. Westerman Jr. of the Pearl Harbor Survivors Association in Atlanta, Georgia, had hoped to take the momentous step of meeting some of the Japanese pilots who took part in the attack, by inviting them to the USA. His plan was vetoed by the national leaders of the association.

4. See the other person as worth forgiving

It's understandable, perhaps, that someone who'd stood on the deck of an American warship at Pearl Harbor would feel reluctant to forgive men who gunned down his colleagues without warning and in cold blood. Imagine such a thing happening to your loved ones, and you'll see just how easily we arrive at the conclusion that some offences are, quite simply, unforgivable.

At the same time, though, people who have endured terrible oppressions sometimes insist on stepping aside from vengeance. In South Africa, for instance, Archbishop Desmond Tutu, who chaired the Truth and Reconciliation Commission, reminds us that:

> *There are people in South Africa who have committed the most unbelievable atrocities, and I am willing for their deeds to be labelled with the harshest epithets: monstrous, diabolical, even devilish. However, monstrous deeds do not turn the perpetrators into monsters. A human person does not ultimately lose his or her humanity, which is characterised by the divine image in which every individual is created... The premise underlying the commission is that it is possible for people to change...*[9]

By 'divine image,' Tutu does not mean that all people, even torturers, are fundamentally decent – only that they are redeemable. There is a distinction between evil deeds and people who commit evil deeds. Yes, it's possible to corrupt yourself, to break down the inhibitions that keep you from seriously antisocial behaviour. But even the worst and most damaged individuals have simply driven their cart into a ditch. They can, in theory, be pulled out again.

Your experiences of being wronged are unlikely to be on this sort of scale. Much hurt occurs not through calculated malice, but through misunderstanding, ineptitude and laziness.

One way to take a more objective view is simply to try and see things from the other person's perspective. The pressures he or she is under. How your behaviour may have come across. How the circumstances behind the hurt arose. None of this excuses the wrong – but it's likely to help you resolve the issue in a more constructive way.

5. Look at the values you're standing on

Here's a controversial thought to finish on. And yet it really has implications not just for forgiveness, but for the whole enterprise of taking the R option.

Whether we're aware of it or not, everything we do expresses a system of values. These values have a number of sources. In part, we consciously adopt them. In part, our parents and other mentors drum them into us. In part, we just soak them up willy-nilly from the way we see other people behaving, either in person or indirectly through the media.

These values are often contradictory or muddled – as shown, for example, in the way we apply more stringent standards to other people's behaviour than we do to our own. Nevertheless, as we go about the business of living, we can often feel these values – these do-this-not-that instincts – running like tramlines underneath us.

So far as forgiveness goes, there are two sets of tramlines, pointing in two opposite directions.

One set points away from reconciliation, and towards the idea that wrongs committed against you justify withdrawal or revenge. In Western postmodern liberalism, the priority given to notions like justice, equality and individual rights means that you yourself decide when, or when not, to forgive. No higher ethic urges or compels you to forgive, say, the terrorist whose activity has resulted in injury to a family member. Indeed, forgiving in situations like that is rare enough to be newsworthy.

Stirring New Age mysticism into the mix doesn't much change this, mainly because New Age is a lifestyle religion and poses no real challenge to the ethic of choice. You forgive a person if you care for him or her. If you don't care, there's little motive to forgive. Better to pull out and start over.

Islam sits on the same tramlines, but operates at the level of family and community. Allah is merciful – though perhaps not reliably so[10] – only to those who surrender. Accordingly, the pattern in traditional Islamic communities tends to be that of forgiveness within a close circle defined by blood or religious affinity, and of militant unforgiveness towards traitors and infidels.

By contrast, the other set of tramlines points away from withdrawal and revenge, and towards the goal of reconciliation. And here the Jewish and Christian traditions are unique in seeing the universe primarily in terms of the restoring of broken relationships.

Christianity's much-misunderstood doctrine of the Trinity puts relationship at the heart of reality by placing it within the very nature of God: three persons, one being. History, from the Christian viewpoint, begins from the breakage of the relationship between humanity and God – Adam and Eve's expulsion from the Garden of Eden. It then moves through the restoration of that relationship by God's self-sacrificial death in the person of Jesus Christ, and on to the fulfilment of that relationship in a new order beyond the present world.

It can be argued – rightly – that Christianity as a religion has presided over a good many massacres and acts of political oppression. Nevertheless, the spirit of the faith – as opposed to the policies of those who like to associate themselves with it – continues to suffuse Western culture with the idea that forgiveness can redeem.

Being forgiven yourself, it becomes possible to forgive even your abusers. There is a wider picture – wider in the sense of falling mostly outside the boundaries of observable reality – in which, according to the Christian faith, the act of forgiving aligns you with something far greater than you see.

It's no coincidence, we think, that reconciliation in South Africa has been built on specifically Christian principles. Reconciliation rests on a base of values in which the rescuing of relationships is not only possible but necessary. All relationships go wrong – between individuals, between communities, between nations. To survive and prosper we must know how to put them right.

1　Reported in the *Guardian*, 8 January 2000.
2　Donald W. Shriver Jr, *An Ethic for Enemies: Forgiveness in Politics* (New York: Oxford University Press, 1995), p.6.
3　For a discussion of the idea of 'total forgiveness' see R.T. Kendall, *Total Forgiveness* (London: Hodder & Stoughton, 2001), p.16. We are grateful to the author for allowing us to read an advance copy of the manuscript.
4　Quoted in David Augsburger, *Caring Enough to Not Forgive* (California: Regal Books, 1981), p.13.
5　David Augsburger, *op.cit.*, pp.9–10.

6   Though often condemned as 'treacherous', Japan's attack on Pearl Harbor was in fact preceded by a formal declaration of war. Japan intended to signal its intentions thirty minutes before the attack. For unforeseen reasons, word did not reach Washington until two hours after.

7   In 1991 a *New York Times* poll showed that 40% of Americans believed Japan should apologise for Pearl Harbor. Significantly, so did 55% of Japanese. As for the Americans apologising for Hiroshima, this was supported by only 16% of Americans and 73% of Japanese. Cited in Donald W. Shriver Jr, *op.cit.*, p.144.

8   Donald Shriver, *ibid.* p.139.

9   Quoted by Trudy Grovier, 'Forgiveness and the Unforgivable', in *American Philosophical Quarterly,* Volume 36, Number 1, January 1999, p.64.

10 Note that the idea of presumption – of being certain of your acceptance by God – is a contentious issue within Islam.

CHAPTER THIRTEEN

ROOTS

Recently I (David) visited the Taj Mahal. It was a commercial tour, which meant you were taken to a souvenir shop on the way back. Not wanting to load up with small plaster replicas of the great monument, I chatted to one of the numerous sales assistants – a teenager with an eager smile – and asked about his career plans. Did he want to set up his own business, or perhaps develop his career with larger retailers in nearby Delhi?

He looked perplexed. 'I am going to work here for the rest of my life', he replied.

WHY WE HAVE TO KEEP MOVING

Looking back, it was a daft question. Despite India's vast size, life in much of it is still essentially local. You tend to live in the same place, doing the same thing, among the same people, till the end of your life. As a result, communities are very strong. There's a lot less money around – but a much richer social environment.

In countries like Britain and the USA, most people have got used to something rather different. In the year 1998–99, 16 per cent of the US population moved home – 17.6 per cent of them to a different state.[1] Percentages for the UK are lower. Nevertheless, just over two per cent of Britons – 1,359,000 people – changed regions in the year 1999.[2] Another survey for the same period shows that 36 per cent of households in the UK had been at their current address for less than five years.[3] That means that a large proportion of the UK population have neighbours today who are not the same as those they had five years ago.

Not all moves are long-distance. Two-thirds of Britons can still say they live within five miles of the place where they were born and raised.[4] But in comparison to a society like that of India, there's a lot more churning in the form of population movement.

One prominent cause of migration in the UK is simply the breaking and reforming of households – between them accounting for 16 per cent of moves.[5] Another – peculiar to the UK – is the effect of Britain's 'boarding school universities'. In countries like France and Australia, most students attend nearby institutions and live at home to minimise accommodation costs. In Britain, however, the past system of maintenance grants has encouraged a different pattern. Students move to a different city to study, and not infrequently stay there to work. In fact, in Sheffield an agency has been set up with the specific aim of 'capturing' graduates for Yorkshire companies, with a special focus on Sheffield's universities.

A more widespread influence, though, and one that's growing in importance with globalisation, is that of the job market. Capital zips around the world so quickly now that demand for your particular skill may swiftly subside in one place and soar in another. Consequently, to get a better and higher-paying position – or perhaps just to get off unemployment benefits – you may find yourself moving from Seattle to Philadelphia, or from Newcastle to Swindon.

To some extent, job mobility has itself become a credential. There's currently an unwritten rule in London, for example, that real high-fliers won't stay in a job longer than three years. In addition, many corporations and public services still maintain a policy of 'training by moving around'. This is less marked than it was – partly because dual-income families are far harder to move. Nevertheless, there are organisations where it survives intact – not least in Britain's National Health Service.

MOBILITY: THE DOWNSIDE

It's proverbially true that young single adults are less 'tied down' than older people with families. But this freedom exacts its own social cost. It often becomes necessary for a circle of friends to take on the supportive role otherwise performed by family (just look at the

American comedy series *Friends*). But such a support network can be vulnerable in a move. Even your live-in partner will not always opt to sacrifice a job and go with you.

In contrast, migrants with families are able to carry their most supportive relationships around with them – at least in theory. But taking your spouse and children with you in a move also spreads the problem around and creates other sources of stress – stress over new schools, lost friends, unfamiliar routines, difficulties finding work. And the likely effect is that your stress will be magnified by the stress of those close to you.

Does time heal? The answer is: yes, but only slowly. Social scientists estimate that it takes at least five years to integrate fully into a new area. If you move on before that time, you will be hard-pressed to form or sustain the kind of long-term relationships through which you can contribute significantly to, say, local politics, a parent and toddler group, or a church.

Nor will short-term relationships be good for much in situations of real need. Talking over the fence with neighbours is one thing. Getting help if you fall seriously ill or are bereaved is quite another. And in real life these things *can* suddenly happen.

KEEPING YOUR ROOTS IN A MOBILE SOCIETY

It's important to balance things up here. After all, plenty of people negotiate changes of job and home without disaster. And a change of situation can – and should – be liberating, romantic, enlightening, and stimulating.

For mobility to deliver those benefits, though, you need to keep in touch with your roots. Having roots isn't the same as being sedentary or stuck. It's having stability across a range of relationships from which you derive on-going emotional and practical support.

Longstanding communities tend to develop this naturally. It should not surprise us that, in an influential study of community in America, Robert Putnam concludes that:

> *Social connectedness is a much stronger predictor of the perceived quality of life in a community than the community's income or educational level. In the five communities surveyed*

having the highest social trust, 52 per cent of residents rated their community as an excellent place to live, the highest possible grade. In the five communities with the lowest levels of social trust, only 31 per cent felt that good about their quality of life. Similarly, personal happiness is also much more closely tied to the level of community social connectedness and trust than to income or educational levels ...Even comparing two persons of identical income, education, race, age, and so on, the one living in a high social capital community typically reports greater personal happiness than his/her 'twin' living in a low social capital community.[6]

The challenge, in a mobile society that forces you to leave significant people behind, is to maintain your 'social connectedness' even when you're on the move. In relationship terms, your roots will spread in many directions. Allowing for some overlap, there are seven main categories:

- home-sharing family (spouse/partner, children, parents, siblings)

- wider family (parents, grandparents, grown children, siblings, uncles and aunts)

- friends

- peers and colleagues

- mentors and teachers

- immediate neighbours

- local service providers.

Building roots requires on-going two-way traffic in relationships, to the point where you enjoy a certain level of mutual trust. Your mother can be relied on to look after your kids for the weekend, just as you can be relied on to help with shopping or clearing out the gutters. You establish strong enough links with your neighbours that you can ask them to feed the cat while you're on holiday. And so on.

Emotional support can be communicated quite effectively without being geographically close. Phone, email, fast roads and low airfares all help keep us 'in touch' without being permanently close.

The greater challenge when you're mobile is to maintain physical contact. Some forms of practical support rely heavily on two bodies being in the same place – things like helping do the decorating, walking the dog, going to the shops, getting to a clinic.

This is true of the workplace as much as it is of family and friends. Of 684 Institute of Management members surveyed in 1999, only 16 per cent expressed a desire to work from home, and only five per cent wanted to telework. The reason? In most cases, simply that being physically present with colleagues both helps their performance on the job and prevents them from feeling marginalised.[7]

It's also true – particularly for older people – that much of life's richness lies in being with family and friends. The weekly phone call may not be enough to make another person feel loved and supported – especially if the person finds travel difficult and thus remains dependent on other people's effort and initiative.

This is why retirement often faces you with a difficult choice between staying where you've been living for the last ten or twenty years – and thus where your friends are – or relocating close to relatives (often children) and leaving your friends, neighbours, and familiar surroundings behind.

Putting down roots will almost inevitably involve tough decisions about location. You don't have to stay in one town from cradle to grave. But you have to be realistic about the constraints location places on your ability to maintain relationships, and you may have to compromise creatively when work and social relationships begin to pull you in opposite directions.

TAKING THE R OPTION WITH ROOTS

The R option in roots begins with being aware of the relationships through which most of the important business of your life is transacted – the relationships that form what you might call your 'relational base'.[8]

Usually, the more mobile you are, the harder it will be to maintain face-to-face contact with significant others. Also, the more mobile you are, the fewer significant others there are likely to be. If you want an instant snapshot of how strong your 'relational base' is, just ask yourself how many people you could call on for sustained help in the event of a crisis – say, a close family member falling ill.

As the term implies, you can't put down roots overnight. It takes time, because building relationships takes time. But it can be done.

1. Think positively about new relationships

Some time ago, a house near ours on the west side of Cambridge was sold, and a new couple moved in. I (Michael) remember discussing with my wife whether or not we should make the effort of getting to know our new neighbours. In the end, we decided not to. Briefly, our reasoning ran as follows. Getting to know people is a time-consuming business. The chances were high that this new couple would themselves soon move on, after which we would, in all probability, never see them again. So what was the point?

As it happened, things turned out just as predicted. Two years later, the couple sold up and left. However, I later told this story at a meeting, to support a point about time-management. I was surprised when a friend in Britain's Foreign Office challenged me on it. What he said was this: 'If everyone made that kind of calculation, the lives of many Foreign Office employees would be miserable. They would never develop friends. In the Foreign Office, you have to move every three years from one country to another. You rely heavily on people being willing to develop these short-term relationships in order to have any kind of quality of life.'

I'm not advocating acts of charity towards employees of the Foreign Office – who in any case are unlikely to be living next door to you. The point is that most of us, seeing so many new faces day after day, just don't bother to make the effort with neighbours. One in three Britons has never even met the person living next door.[9]

One advantage of moving, in relational terms, is that at least it offers the opportunity of a new start. Changing location will tend to shake down your relationships. You'll keep up the ones that matter most to you, and the others you'll let drop – which in turn gives room to look for new ones. People with children sometimes have an advantage here, if only because the role of parent forces some new relationships on you – with school staff and other parents. But Internet sites that index local community groups are making it easier to find people who share your interests – and thus to put down roots in a new area.

2. Be cautious of opt-in community

Putting down roots, though, implies a movement beyond the immediate and the superficial. One of the things you may want to think about in the R option is just how supportive your supportive relationships are.

Mobility has seen to it that community of the *Coronation Street* kind is in decline. Increasingly we look at community with a consumer's eye – seeking something that fits our needs exactly. If the fit isn't good enough – or if we run into conflicts and clashes of personality – we feel free to move on. By running our social lives in this way, we preserve a sense of 'feel-good' without having the inconvenience of getting too close to other people's pain. But while feel-good is fine, it won't in itself establish the kinds of relationship that are helpful when things go wrong.

Professional associations are a case in point. Increasingly touted as a source of community, professional groupings of lawyers, accountants, or architects are, in reality, communities of convenience. If illness forces you into premature retirement, your fellow members won't be coming round to help mow your lawn.

3. Assess job and house moves in terms of relationships

Getting a new job and moving to new accommodation are both major life-changes. Making choices in these areas, we usually look at financial issues first: salary, purchase cost, terms and conditions, value for money, promotion prospects, investment potential. And so on.
Looking at the R option, however, it's clear that changes in work and housing have important implications for our relationships. Further, when we change job or move to a new house, we are in effect making strategic decisions with consequences that will follow us for years to come. It's worth getting them right.

In the R option, then, you may want to assess a new job opportunity with questions like these:

- What benefits to my relationships are made possible by this increase in pay? Or, how might relational benefits outweigh the drop in salary?

- What will the location of the job, and its associated travelling, do to my ability to maintain and build relationships that matter to me?

- What sort of relational environment does the job provide?

- What demands will the work make that may conflict with my commitment to relationships with partner and family?

- Will I have sufficient support to cope with work-related stress?

- From the relationships point of view, is this job a step forward from my current position?

- Will taking this job entail disruption in the lives of those close to me – for instance, changes of school or employer?

A similar set of questions can be asked about house moves – which often go along with a change of job.

- How will this move affect my distance from family and friends?

- How will the move affect my journey to work – and what consequences will this have for my relating time?

- How will the move affect others in the household – a partner in work, or children at school or playgroup?

- What kind of architectural environment am I moving into, and how will variables like number of bedrooms or garden affect relationships in the house?

- How close is the new accommodation to playgrounds, parks and other leisure facilities important to relaxation and relationship building?

- If I have children, what quality of social environment does the neighbourhood provide – for instance, are there other children of comparable age?

- How easy will it be to maintain previous relationships, and what potential does the new location offer for forming new relationships?

- Is the local community receptive to incomers – or is the idyllic village likely to turn into a social nightmare?

- Are there facilities in the house for keeping guests, or having relatives to stay?

Admittedly, there are problems with the ideal of achieving family co-location. Should you live near your side of the family, or your partner's side?

You might also ask whether it's worth trying to meet your potential neighbours before you commit to buying a house. Finding a mechanism for doing this isn't easy. Nevertheless, the position of your house determines to a large extent who it is you'll be mixing with in your local area. Just as important, if you have a family, it determines who it is your children will be mixing with.

4. Look forward 20, 30, 40 years

On one occasion, I (Michael) had a conversation about roots with the manager of one of the large retail stores in Edinburgh, Scotland. He was having difficulty because his elderly parents lived in the South-East of England – some four hundred miles away – and he wanted to be close to them to give them the kind of support and help they needed. Being based in Edinburgh made the fulfilment of these family obligations extremely difficult. He now wished, he told me, that he had planned his career differently. If he had only thought ahead, and had foreseen the needs his parents would have at this stage of life, he could have planned his career within the store group so that he would have been working closer to them.

When he was younger, however, he'd had no concept of roots, and simply hadn't bothered to think about the long-term needs of his parents or other members of his family. The result was that he now felt guilty that he couldn't meet his parents' needs – despite the frustration, and financial and time cost, of trying to see them as much as he could.

Relationships, by nature, are long-term assets. You can offload them easily, but you can't buy them. And consequently, it's worth remembering that strategic decisions you make today will continue to have consequences for your relationships twenty, thirty and forty years down the line.

Some of the questions you can ask yourself in strategic decision-making are as follows.

- How easy will it be to keep in touch with friends?

- If I don't have job security or a skill I can use from home (as in teleworking), am I close to a centre where there will be a range of suitable job opportunities? If so, this may save a disrupting move if I lose my present job.

- Where do I want to be at times in the future when close members of my family might need my help – or I might need theirs?

- Where can I locate so that my children can have a satisfactory secondary education, and the option of taking further education without being forced to leave home?

- In what places can I and my partner both find work, and maintain and develop networks of significant social support?

- Where can I locate such that my own children have the opportunity of working and settling within a reasonable distance?

5. Build a 'relational pension'

Commercials for pension funds usually push two messages. The first – explicitly the concern of the advertiser – is that with the right kind of investment you can enjoy a long, healthy and prosperous retirement. The second is that you have someone to share it with. Thus commercials of this kind routinely show a sprightly old couple enjoying the rewards of lifelong prudence *together.*

In reality things are rather different. Prosperous or not, an enormous number of elderly people in Britain end up living on their own. Overall the trend has been away from family care and towards institutionalisation. It's estimated that between 1991 and 1996 the numbers involved in informal caring in the UK fell from 6.1 million to 5.7 million – a change explained in part by pressures on women to contribute to household finances.[10] It's just a fact that, in a mobile society, the older members are the most likely to be neglected. And sooner or later, that means you.

Planners put much faith in videoconferencing. 'Each Sunday I will be able to walk into my sitting room, switch on the equipment and have breakfast with my mother, even though we are 200 miles apart.'[11] If a disembodied breakfast meets your social needs, or your mother's, then fine. I suspect, though, that it won't. And the only alternative to a relationally impoverished old age is to build the networks of contemporary and cross-generational relationships throughout your life that will sustain you in later years.

A relational pension – preparing for later years by building long-term relationships that will last into old age – may sound a strange device. And it could be argued that (life being what it is) relational pensions are vulnerable to outside forces, just as financial investments are affected by vagaries of the market. On the other hand, risk doesn't dampen our belief in saving. And relationships – carefully chosen, well spread, and continually paid into – will usually offer impressive returns.

---

1   Source: *US Census*, Current Population Survey: Geographical Mobility (Update) March 1998 to March 1999, at: http://www.census.gov/prod/2000pubs/p20-531.pdf
2   Source: *Social Trends 2001* Table 1-12, p.36. (Social Trends no.31, London: Office for National Statistics).
3   Source: *Regional Trends Dataset, 1998–1999* 'Households: by length of time at current address', ONS ref. RT35607. From Regional Trends 35, 2000 Edition. At: http://www.statistics.gov.uk.
4   Statistic from the *Sunday Times*, quoted in *The Week*, 23 December 2000, p.22.
5   Source: Social Trends, *op. cit.*, Table 10-17, p.185.
6   See Robert D. Putnam, *Bowling Alone: Collapse and Revival of American Community* (New York: Simon & Schuster, 2000). Much of the data behind the book is available on the website: www.bettertogether.org.
7   See Michael Moynagh and Richard Worsley, *Understanding The Present By Thinking About The Future* (London: The Tomorrow Project, 2000), p.19.
8   For a discussion of this concept, see the first chapter of Nicola Baker (ed), *Building a Relational Society* (Aldershot: Arena, 1996). This book can be ordered for £15 plus P & P from the Relationships Foundation or through its website (www.relationshipsfoundation.org/books/Index.html).
9   Statistic from the *Sunday Times*, *op.cit.*, p.22
10 Michael Moynagh and Richard Worsley, *op.cit.*, pp.96, 97.
11 Michael Moynagh and Richard Worsley, *op.cit.*, p.97.

CHAPTER FOURTEEN

HEALTH

A few weeks ago, I (David) had one of those moments that parents dread. My daughter came to the front door with blood streaming out of her mouth. She'd fallen over, whacked her face on the pavement, and dislodged one of her front teeth. It was seven o'clock on a Saturday evening – not an ideal time to be finding a dentist. We scrambled to find a surgery still open, and set off at high speed to reach it.

Looking back, I think what I most feared was irreparable damage – something happening to her that couldn't be put right. I found myself giving her assurances that were really assurances to myself. Dentists are very clever now. They can repair broken teeth. Even if a tooth falls out they can put another one in so it looks just like it did before. None of which, I'm sure, she felt comforted by, or even heard.

I would not care to repeat the hour that followed – a child who is scared at the mere sight of a needle having to undergo emergency dental surgery. But we came out, a little shaken up, with the tooth pushed back in and splinted to its neighbour with a resin adhesive. I was able to give her a hug and say – again, as much to myself as to her – 'Don't worry, it's okay, it's all going to be all right.'

What we'd experienced was a very particular kind of medicine – the kind practised throughout the Western world and idealised in television dramas like *ER*. Its technical name is *biomedicine*. The essence of it is intervention and repair. Sticking back loose teeth is the kind of technological fix it excels at. Like a car, you get towed in, you get tinkered with, you drive out.

I have reason to be grateful to the thousands of people whose research and expertise has made possible emergency dental surgery.

And I recognise that technology has more miracles up its sleeve. Open-heart surgery is now almost routine. Given time and funding – and a bit of luck – new and better fixes will be found for conditions like paraplegia, Alzheimer's, and cancer.

And yet from a relationships standpoint, there are two serious problems with biomedicine – problems, ironically, rooted in its very success.

MEDICINE AS BREAKDOWN RECOVERY

Neal Nunnelly served on the *USS Anzio* towards the end of the Second World War. He later wrote his memoirs, recalling a particular visit the 'Big A' made to China:

> *They lined us up and gave us cholera shots and then sailed up the Yangtze and Wang Poo rivers to Shanghai. We arrived in November 1945 and stayed a number of weeks so had an opportunity to see it well. I hate to say this, but an awful lot of Chinese girls got screwed while the Big A was there. Didn't we have fun? Yes. Because penicillin was now available, the gonorrhoea epidemic, better known by its more endearing term, 'The Clap', was quickly quelled. After all, a couple million units of that mouldy stuff in your fat butt was a piece of cake.*[1]

The discovery of penicillin must count among the greatest achievements of biomedicine in the twentieth century. But as Nunnelly's story shows, the new treatment had a double edge.

Apart from the exploitative and degrading way in which these Chinese women were treated, it's clear that the ability of penicillin to cure sexually transmitted disease made the naval ratings *less* careful in avoiding infection. If they got the Clap, all they had to do was go back to the ship for a jab. In effect, the cure created its own epidemic.

The psychology of this extends far beyond the US Navy. We all have a habit of treating medical technology as a kind of safety net. The more convenient or alluring the lifestyle that makes us ill, the more the all-singing-all-dancing capability of medicine to put things right starts to figure in our calculations.

As a nation we like eating red meat and crisps, drinking too much, sitting in armchairs, and smoking. It's easier to believe we're going to get away with it than it is to knuckle down to the dull business of keeping ourselves healthy. And as a result, inexpensive prevention gets muscled aside by the big-budget technology of cure.

BEING THE BATTLEFIELD

The second problem with biomedicine is quite different, and concerns the way doctors and patients interrelate.

Think back to the last time you visited a hospital consultant. You were sick, perhaps without knowing the reason. You were in the unfamiliar environment of an emergency or outpatients department. How did you feel?

Possibly you felt anxious, vulnerable. Probably you felt faintly envious of the consultant, who seemed fit and healthy and could walk out of the hospital after work and leave all the illness behind. Probably you felt oppressed by the medical hardware you'd always supposed was for use on other people, and not on you.

These feelings are not a kind of background music that fades up, willy-nilly, whenever you're seriously ill. They are a response to the way biomedicine relates the doctor to the patient.

Treatment in biomedicine, which ought to be an encounter between people, is reduced instead to a contest between doctor and disease. You are merely the battleground, an example of your illness, a 'disease specimen'.[2] Your role in treatment is only to acquiesce while the technology – chemotherapy, antibiotics, electroconvulsive therapy – flushes the sickness out. Healing is something done to you.

Because this way of connecting doctor, patient and disease is deeply rooted in biomedicine, it's hard for doctors to frame the relationship in any other way. Biomedicine will shape your expectations as well as the doctor's behaviour. And it has to be said that biomedical training doesn't attach much importance to even the most obvious relational issues, like bedside manner.

Yet the relationship between patient and doctor is crucial. Even laser treatment and microsurgery are pretty crude instruments. In the end, even the most advanced medical practitioners rely heavily on your body's ability to heal itself. And in this process, your sense of confidence and involvement are big assets. You *ought* to be able to walk into a consultant's office – even be stretchered in – and feel that you and the doctor are partners, working together in the process of your body's self-healing.

In fact, medicine should be taking account of relationships in three very basic areas – not just when you get towed into the repair shop.

ILLNESS IS A RELATIONAL CONDITION, NOT JUST A PHYSIOLOGICAL ONE

The unpleasantness of being ill derives to a large extent from the fact that you can't participate in normal work and social relationships. You feel too sick to go out and do the things you usually do. And if people come to see you, you no longer feel quite on a par with them. You sense that they're doing you a favour by visiting you when you're laid up.

This isn't so bad if the illness is temporary. But if it drags on, your links with your social networks may be loosened, and you may start to feel uncomfortable about imposing on those who care for you. It's sobering to ask yourself how many of your regular social contacts – the ones from whom you derive a sense of self-worth – would survive in their present form if you lost your legs or got a serious cancer.

Once you're out of childhood, being dependent on somebody else takes a toll on both sides of the relationship. The dependent person feels a burden; the helper senses the weight.

BAD AND BROKEN RELATIONSHIPS DAMAGE YOUR HEALTH

There's an enormous body of literature now on stress-related illness. Stress arises in unsatisfactory relations – between bosses and employees, between partners, between a person who wants affection and another who refuses to give it.

A lot of routine stress arises from relationships at work, through overload, time pressure, repetitive tasks and role conflict. Major

disorders resulting from stress include: hypertension, coronary throm-
bosis, allergies, asthma, pruritis, peptic ulcers, constipation, rheu-
matoid arthritis, nervous dyspepsia, depression, diabetes, skin
disorders, and colitis.[3]

Writing on emotional intelligence, Daniel Goleman points out that
the link between stress and ill-health now forms the basis of a leading medical subdiscipline called PNI, or psychoneuroimmunology.[44]

Some of the main findings to emerge are these:

- **Stress taxes your body indirectly** It's generally accepted that stress
  can make you eat too much, eat too little, hit the bottle, or
  increase your consumption of cigarettes. But just as much damage is done when stress causes anger and aggression. An eight-
  year study of 1,012 heart-attack victims by Stanford University
  Medical School showed that aggressive men suffered the highest
  rates of second heart attacks. A Yale study of 929 men showed
  that those considered as easily roused to anger were three times
  more likely to die of cardiac arrest than those considered even-
  tempered. Anger and hostility, then, appear to be among the factors causing coronary artery disease.[5]

- **Stress lowers immune resistance** A classic study by Sheldon Cohen
  of Carnegie-Mellon University assessed the stress levels being
  experienced by a sample group, and then exposed them all to the
  same strain of cold virus. He found that the people with the more
  stressed lives were more likely to catch the cold. Only 27 per cent
  of those with low stress caught the infection. Among those suffering high stress, the figure was 47 per cent. Comparable studies
  have shown that, for example, married couples who have gone
  through upsetting events like marital fights were more likely to
  come down with a cold or upper respiratory infection.[6]

- **Isolation causes higher mortality rates** Twenty-year studies involving
  37,000 people indicate that social isolation – the sense that you
  have nobody to share your private feelings with or be close to –
  doubles your chances of sickness or death. In 1987, *Science* concluded that isolation was as significant to mortality rates as smoking, high blood pressure, high cholesterol, obesity and lack of
  physical exercise. In fact, social isolation is more likely to kill you
  than smoking.[7]

STAY CONNECTED, STAY FIT

You recover from illness faster and more fully when you have supportive relationships around you. The reasons aren't hard to work out.

First, relationships help you comply with your medical regime. Taking the tablets regularly, eating the right things, and not 'overdoing it' are easier when somebody else is there to nag or encourage you.

Second, being supported relationally plays a key role in boosting your morale and keeping depression at bay.[8]

And third, other people are just an immense practical help. Your local doctor may prescribe rest – but you won't get much if there isn't somebody there to make your bed, cook your meals and assist with shopping.

A Swedish study published in 1993 examined the changing medical condition of 752 men as they aged from 53 to 60. One striking discovery was that, although 41 of the men died during the study period, among those who claimed to have a dependable network of close relationships – wife, close friends, children – there was no connection at all between high stress levels and death rate.[9] Close relationships, in other words, are good for health.

Similarly, there's a link between emotional support and resistance to cancer. Dr. David Spiegel, of Stanford University Medical School, studied women with advanced metastatic breast cancer. Those who had nobody to unburden themselves to lived, on average, nineteen months after treatment. Those who joined weekly meetings with fellow women patients – meetings where they could speak freely about their fear, pain and anger, and be listened to – lived, on average, thirty-seven months. The difference could not be explained by any difference in medical treatment.[10]

TAKING THE R OPTION IN HEALTH

At the turn of the millennium, the Gallup organisation polled 50,000 people around the world and asked them 'What matters most in life?'. By far the most common responses were 'Good health' (43 per cent, first in 37 out of 60 countries) and 'A happy family life' (41 per cent, first in 16 countries).[11]

The two, of course, are closely connected. Taking the R option in health, though, means more than having close family on hand – though having strong relationships at the centre of your 'relational base' both reduces your chance of being ill, and increases your prospects of survival and recovery. Among the ideas you may want to consider are the following.

1. Think through the impact of your illness on other people

Health isn't just a possession, or an asset, or a privilege; it's also a responsibility. To some extent this idea is embedded in the culture. Most of us were instructed as children to 'Cover your mouth when you cough'. But we're far from consistent in applying the principle. In Japan, it's considered antisocial to travel on the underground when you have a cold. In Britain – parental advice notwithstanding – it's macho to turn up at work even if you're running a temperature of 105.

A related area you may want to look at is taking a balanced approach to risk. For example, are you being fair to your partner or children if you fail to change your lifestyle after having a heart attack? Similarly – at a far earlier stage – where does the balance lie between the needs of those who depend on you, and your own need to, say, work all hours, drink heavily, race motorcycles, or go skydiving?

The point is that personal lifestyle decisions have a relational angle. There's a place for risk-taking and living on the edge. There's also a place for making tomorrow's health needs register in today's decision-making. Reconciling the two is another aspect of self-management.

When other people depend on you, emotionally or financially, health is no longer simply 'your own business'. The woman whose husband is fifty-five, overweight and a heavy smoker has a right to feel her interests are being sidelined. He may be condemning her to spend her later years without the companionship and support she'd counted on.

2. Aim for parity in your relationship with your doctor

It would help if we could treat doctors like lawyers or accountants – expert advisors in matters for which we ourselves bear ultimate responsibility. In Britain, one of the reasons we don't is that doctors, unlike lawyers and accountants, are paid for by the state. They are autonomous professionals – and too often we respond to this by treating them as gurus.[12]

This isn't helped by the conditions in which doctors have to work. For example, your family practitioner functions as a carer as well as a therapist. But this caring role has to be carried out during short, infrequent meetings held in the unconducive setting of the surgery. And that's assuming you even see the same doctor on consecutive visits.

Given this background, your relationship with the doctor will tend to go one of two ways. On the one hand, and particularly when the illness is serious, you may start to slip into an attitude of dependency. You may feel that the doctor's experience so far outweighs your own that he, or she, should be left to take control.

When you're on the operating table, of course, your life is literally in a doctor's hands. But away from that particular kind of precipice, leaving *everything* to a doctor's interventions can damage rather than enhance your prospects of achieving good health.

For one thing, in some conditions, like diabetes, success depends to a large extent on how well you manage your treatment when the doctor isn't around. For another, what you might call 'positive mental attitude' appears to have considerable influence on healing – and sometimes does so in defiance of a doctor's prediction that you'll be dead within six months.

On the other hand, it's possible for your relationship with the doctor to slide the other way. In this case, you adopt the role of private or state-sponsored consumer. As such, you'll feel entitled to call the doctor out at three in the morning; entitled to get the prescriptions you want (including antibiotics for colds); and entitled to miss appointments without notice.

In contrast to all this, cultivating a genial and partner-based relationship with your doctor can pay substantial dividends.

For example, a doctor who already understands the background to your pressures at work will be better able to advise you sensibly. Also, there's the matter of effective time use. Having an established relationship with your doctor usually enables you to communicate more efficiently and with less risk of misunderstanding.

And there's nothing wrong with informing yourself. If you use a medical encyclopaedia or the Internet to read up on your symptoms, you'll have more chance of understanding the doctor's diagnosis and of asking the right questions. Reading doesn't make you an expert, but it enables you to make better use of expert advice.

3. Think how you support others when they're ill

We often have a knee-jerk reaction to other people's illness. We send a card, or buy some flowers, possibly make a visit. All of which is fine as far as it goes. But where someone's illness is prolonged, you may want to think through how you can most effectively contribute the support he or she needs. Partly this just comes down to consistency. The first bunch of flowers will be appreciated. The second, a week later, will show that your concern goes beyond a token gesture.

Having friends nearby can make a substantial difference to a patient's sense of wellbeing. Medical staff usually do not have time to sit down and talk, provide books and magazines, or bring a tooth-brush and a change of pyjamas.

Even more important, people weakened by illness or advancing years need relatives and friends to act as advocates for them. In a medical crisis, you often don't know what's going on around you. And even if you're lucid, you may not be in a physical or emotional state to press for your needs to be met.

I (Michael) was recently told about an elderly woman in hospital whose meal tray was efficiently delivered and taken away – without anyone noticing she hadn't eaten. She had grown too weak to feed herself. Had it not been for her daughter, who saw what was going on and reported it to the nursing staff, the woman would literally have died of starvation.

The greater the pressure on the health service, the more important it becomes for a patient's family and friends not only to provide practical and emotional support, but to track the patient's progress.

4. Get fit in company

We often get into the habit of exercising alone. If you have a ski-track or a rowing machine, you'll probably be watching the news or listening to tapes rather than holding a conversation. In repetitive exercise, multitasking can relieve the boredom. But exercise can provide an opportunity to build relationships. Walking to the shops brings you into proximity with neighbours in a way that car travel inhibits. Going to a gym is as much an excuse to socialise as going for a drink at a pub.

As a friend said to me recently about his early morning jogging in America, 'It added a different dimension to my neighbourhood relationships. Previously they'd been limited to chatting while we watched our children attempt to play baseball.'

5. Avoid using biomedical treatment as a 'fix'

I (Michael) have a friend who once used strong anti-migraine drugs. The drugs had the severe side-effect of making him cough, and on one occasion, at a dinner party, brought on such a bad coughing fit that he ruptured his oesophagus. Had it not been that a doctor was at the table with him, he probably would have died.

He only took the drugs because the migraines were so painful. But then, he probably only had the migraines because he constantly overworked. In other words, there are other, less dangerous options he could have taken to solve his problem – options involving the way he handled relationships in his place of work and in other areas of his life.

There is an argument against this, of course. Outside the area of life-threatening illness (heart disease, for example), many busy people will object that popping pills is simply a way of keeping troublesome symptoms at bay in order to achieve a higher level of productivity. If they have a headache, they take aspirin; they don't go home and lie in a darkened room.

The point we are trying to make is that using biomedicine in this way requires a prediction of outcomes and a weighing of risks. For various reasons, you may find yourself trading-off your long-term health against the demands of your family, profession, or vocation. There's no rule that says you can't burn yourself out for a worthy cause. Nor is there a rule that says you can't make difficult changes – like getting a different job – in order to preserve your health. You need to take a long, hard look at your situation, and decide.

1   Neal Nunnelly, *The Yellow Brick Road Is Longer Than I Thought: Fifteen Years Of Depression And War – A Musical Memoir* (unpublished). This excerpt can found at http://www.historycentral.com/navy/stories/Anzio.html

2   See R.S. Laura and S. Heaney, *Philosophical Foundations of Health Education*, (New York, London: Routledge, 1985), p.67. For this reason, it's important how we name people who are ill. A 'person with diabetes' is different from a 'diabetic'. The first term stresses the person's individuality, the second implies that he or she is notable mainly as an example of a disadvantaged class.

3   See Jill Earnshaw & Cary Cooper, *Stress and Employer Liability* (London: Institute of Personnel and Development, 1996), Table 2, p.9.

4   Daniel Goleman, *Emotional Intelligence: Why It Can Matter More than IQ*, (London: Bloomsbury, 1996), p.167.

5   See Lynda H. Powell, 'Emotional Arousal as a Predictor of Long-Term Mortality and Morbidity in Post M.I. Men,' *Circulation,* Vol.82, No.4, Supplement III, October 1990, p.259.

6   See Sheldon Cohen *et al.*, 'Psychological Stress and Susceptibility to the Common Cold,' in *New England Journal of Medicine,* 325 (1991). Also: Arthur Stone *et al,* 'Secretory IgA as a Measure of Immunocompetence,' in *Journal of Human Stress,* 13 (1987).

7   The difference in mortality risk is 2.0 to 1.6. See James House *et al,* 'Social Relationships and Health,' in *Science,* 29 July 1988.

8   Prevalence of treated depression in the UK is relatively low – around 3% for men, and 7.5% for women (source: NHS General Practice Statistics on www.statistics.gov.uk). However, NHS Direct estimates that, at any one time in the UK, depression affects about 15–30% of people. Over a lifetime, there is a 60–70% chance that you will suffer depression that affects your daily living. This effect is reinforced by medical advances and improvements in living standards, which reduce the impact of physical illnesses like pneumonia and thus cause the relative impact of depression to increase. Depression is already ten times more common in the USA than it was two generations ago (source: Robert Putnam in *Le Monde,* quoted in *The Week,* 9 December 2000). It is estimated that by the year 2020 depression will be the second most common cause of disability in the developed world, and the prime cause in the developing world.

9   See Annika Rosengren *et al.,* 'Stressful Life Events, Social Support, and Mortality in Men Born in 1933,' *British Medical Journal,* 19 October 1993.

10 See David Spiegel *et al.,* 'Effect of Psychosocial Treatment on Survival of Patients with Metastatic Breast Cancer,' *Lancet,* No.8668, ii (1989).

11 Réné Spogard, *World Opinion: A happy family life and good health is what matters most in life,* Gallup International (4 April 2000). Other responses were: a job (23.1%), freedom (16.2%), no violence and corruption (14.0%), standard of living (12.8%), faithfulness to religion (12.6%), and an education (11.6%).

12 Doctor–patient relationships in private healthcare differ in this respect, although private healthcare raises its own relational issues.

CHAPTER FIFTEEN

SCHOOLING

For about one hundred and fifty days every year, I (David) drive my children across the city to their school. There I kiss them, and entrust them to the care of other adults who – in truth – I don't know very well, and whose professional expertise I have no choice but to rely on.

How do I feel? First (I'm being honest), I feel relief. Dearly though I love my children, I know that for the next six hours I can organise my work schedule without having to juggle childcare.

But I also feel concern. The school is good, even excellent. Nevertheless, these little children I leave at the classroom door will probably be among my closest companions until the day I die. I want them to turn out well. I want it for them, and I want it for me. After all, one day I may have to depend on their kindness and good judgement. It matters what the school is teaching them.

None of which would need to be said if the education system – whose influence on your children is immense – were helping those children to be wise, generous, helpful and relationally astute. But despite the efforts of many good schools and many dedicated teachers, the system as a whole often fails to achieve that outcome.

In the UK, at least, this situation has a lot to do with the way government policy on schooling is administered. Many schools fail to deliver, not from a lack of willingness, but because of the burden of competing, and shifting priorities being placed on teachers by the machinery of government above.

So what can you do about it?

RELATIONSHIPS ARE TOMORROW'S SKILL

Note, first of all, that such 'soft' social skills have hard economic value. Out there in the job market, there's a fast-growing demand for people who know how to manage relationships. In 1998, when UK employers were asked by the Association of Graduate Recruiters what they most sought in graduates, they put interpersonal skills and team-working top of the list.[1]

Valerie Bayliss, director of the Redefining Work project, established by Britain's Royal Society of Arts, predicts that future employers will demand the following skills, in this order:

- High-level competence in literacy, numeracy, and IT.

- Knowledge of ethics, values and how society, government and business work.

- Grasp of scientific method and the concept of proof.

- Knowing how to learn new skills and knowledge.

- Knowing how to evaluate and appreciate information.

- Knowing how to take charge of your own learning.

- Knowing how to deal well with, and value, other people.

- Knowing how to communicate effectively with others.

- Knowing how to work in teams.

- Knowing how to cope with approaching change.

- Knowing how to make things change.

- Knowing how to manage risk and uncertainty.

- Knowing how to be assertive enough to get your concerns addressed.

- Knowing how to manage your own time and get results.

- Knowing how to manage your life, including your financial affairs.

- Knowing how to manage your personal and emotional relationships.

- Knowing how to make the best of your creative talents.[2]

Seven out of these seventeen competences are explicitly to do with acquiring high-order interpersonal skills. You may or may not agree with Bayliss's prediction point for point. But the drift towards a greater relationship emphasis is already with us. Professional tasks are becoming more complex, drawing together teams with mixed skills, and thus putting a premium on the ability to work in collaboration.

In the view of American psychologist Daniel Goleman, EQ (emotional intelligence, or monitoring your own and other people's feelings) may be at least as important as IQ in determining a person's life success.[3] Even money management increasingly involves interfacing with others – service providers, public utilities and government agencies.

WHAT YOUR CHILDREN ARE BEING TRAINED TO DO

When our parents were at school in Britain during the 1930s, teachers doled out information in lumps – history, Latin, algebra – and the children either mastered it or went under. Today a teacher is expected to relate to, and cater for, each child as an individual. Children are fruits to be ripened, not chickens to be stuffed.

It's fair to say that the idea of relationships being central to education goes back a very long way. In his Gifford Lectures of 1953 and 1954, the philosopher John Macmurray, who has had such an influence on the UK Prime Minister, Tony Blair, argued that:

The first priority in education – if by education we mean learning to be human – is learning to live in personal relation to other people ... I call this the first priority because failure in this is fundamental failure, which cannot be compensated for by success in other fields.[4]

Certainly in Britain, however, 'success in other fields' seems to have been much on the minds of those framing educational policy.

Primary and secondary curricula, once static and self-defining, increasingly reflect the end-use to which they will be put. In a fast-changing and data-driven age, knowing your Shakespeare may be less useful than knowing how to adapt, solve problems, and acquire new skills. Training for life turns into lifelong learning. Once-and-for-all 'just in case' information gets sidelined in favour of pinpoint skills a person can pick up 'just in time'.[5]

It's no coincidence that this shift is being driven by UK central government. Nor that central government has tightened its grip on the reins of the schooling system. We now have a *national* curriculum, testing for children at age 7, 11, 14 and 16, stripping of powers from teachers and Local Education Authorities, performance league tables. And the unceremonious take-over of failing schools.

Why is education a hot issue? For one simple reason. Top management at UK plc has twigged that staying afloat in the world economy depends on having a highly skilled workforce.

Right now, surveys of our educational attainment are pretty depressing. British school-leavers rank second to bottom in the EU league.[6] The fear is that low school performance will boomerang. Redundancies forced by low-cost competition from abroad will leave more people chasing fewer jobs at the lower end of the market. And that means a larger pool failing to make an adequate living and, therefore, needing the subsidy of tax credits and benefits.

Industry also suffers. British companies will spend more money on training to offset the skills deficit. It will take them longer than their competitors to repair machinery, and they will use new equipment less efficiently. All of which will impact negatively on profit margins and discourage new investment.

No wonder, then, that the government is digging its spurs into the educational system in an effort to raise the pace. Head teachers now have to process an enormous amount of information, in the form of directives and advice – on a wide range of education-related goals. But as workplace demands filter further and further down through the school years, so the attention of teachers and parents alike gets more sharply focused on *academic* achievement.

The gains come at a price. For example, there are clear benefits to individual pupil tracking – but the bureaucratic burden this has imposed makes teachers less able to chat informally, provide pastoral care, or run after-school clubs. Likewise, there are clear benefits to prioritising core skills like literacy and numeracy – but in the zero-sum arithmetic of the school day this means the subjects that teach children how to relate get sidelined.

In the end, how well the child knows the teacher is a powerful determinant of the child's interest in the subject being taught. If the extra pressure on the teacher results in the child feeling ignored, then the relationship is being damaged, with direct implications for the child's motivation and achievement.

It would help, of course, if the need for relational competence were reflected in the way we define academic achievement. For example, given the importance of working in teams, there's a strong argument for making the ability to collaborate a teachable and testable skill.

TAKING THE R OPTION IN SCHOOLING

In the UK, the 1992 Education Act obliges every school to have a policy on spiritual, moral, social and cultural development, and teachers in general take this very seriously.

But this side of their work is under-resourced. Far more of their time and energy goes into the burdensome requirement to track and test performance. On top of which, teachers in many state schools find themselves struggling not only with the challenge of educating children but also with that of controlling the behavioural fall-out from stressed and dysfunctional families.

Against this background, it's all the more important for parents to keep relational issues at the centre of their thinking. Education policy may be determined by central government and driven by global economic forces, but you can still exert a powerful influence on the kind of education your child receives.

1. Do what schools can't

Educationalists sometimes refer to the '80/20 Rule'. It's a statement of the limits schools work within. Although pupils spend an average of 15,000 hours in secondary school, a school will exert only 20 per cent of the total educational influence brought to bear on them. The other 80 per cent is down to parents.

These figures are slightly impressionistic. But there's no doubt that parental influence is fundamental, and to a large extent determinative. It's no good asking a school to turn your children into responsible citizens if your own behaviour models something different. Schools can't give your children values you yourself don't live by – no matter how good they are. They can't reverse damage done by relationships going wrong at home. They're not even the primary influence when it comes to laying the foundations of relationship skill.

For example, 'sex and relationship education' is a vast improvement on 'sex education'. But it's doubtful whether children learn much that's useful about sexuality through instruction in a classroom. They need positive role models, adults they trust enough to confide in, and wider relationships in which they can develop self-confidence and poise.

2. Take care what kind of pressure you exert as a parent

It's an inevitable result of publishing performance league tables that schools will prioritise the outputs the tables measure. But once the government has defined what a 'good' school is, the pressure to emphasise mainly academic achievement is kept up by articulate, ambitious, professional parents. If you're one of them, you may want to think through what it is you'd like *your* child to get out of his or her schooling.

It's not an easy balance to get right. A father who'd moved from Hong Kong asked me (David) recently why, at a British school, his nine-year-old son was getting only half an hour's homework per night. To him, the British educational regime appeared lenient to the point of neglect.

On the other hand, parental angst about academic performance can be debilitating for children. One primary head has complained, 'I no longer have happy children.'[7] Happiness isn't everything. But in children, it's not something we should too readily trade away.

3. Ask the right questions when you select a school

It's not always obvious from the outside how good – or bad – a school is at supporting and teaching relationships. Being top of the performance league table for academic achievement says nothing about the school as a social environment. And conversely, being in the middle of the inner city doesn't prevent a school being disciplined, constructive and caring. But how do you tell?

Well, here are some things to look out for.

- **How far does the school encourage children to relate *between year-groups?*** School children can be very conscious of age and year distinctions. Consequently, a large school may resemble a building where people on one floor have little or no contact with those on another. Schools with a strong awareness of relationships will be giving older children responsibility for younger ones. Some bridge age barriers through 'buddy' schemes, where older children help younger ones to read. Others set up 'listener schemes' in which younger children who are experiencing bullying can talk safely with a responsible older child.

- **Does the school break its student body down into smaller loyalty groups?** A teacher at a large Leicestershire comprehensive school once told me how time pressure had forced the school to abolish its house structure – the system in which pupils of all ages belong to one of four or five smaller units called 'houses'. As a result, he felt, the school had lost much of its social strength. Without houses, for example, there were no end-of-year parties where different age groups could be brought together in manageably small groups. Even in larger schools, plenary assemblies can help in maintaining a sense of corporate identity. But children, like adults, identify better with the 'little platoon' than with a large institution. For that reason, relationally-conscious schools will not treat houses, school councils and clubs as luxuries. These cross-cutting groups reinforce the social cohesion of the school.

- **How do teachers handle relationships in the classroom?** Evidence suggests that teacher–child relationships based on monitoring, child-focused targets and individual attention are beneficial to both sides. But this doesn't mean smaller class sizes are always better. More than thirty may stretch the resources of a single teacher. But if the number falls below twenty, a different problem arises. There are too few sub-groups, and a child ostracised from one sub-group may not be able to fit into another. Class dynamics are also important. Where you sit pupils in a classroom affects both the way they relate and the way they learn. Boys are more subject to peer pressure, and more likely to play up if they don't think learning is 'cool'. Aware of this, one North London secondary school achieves stronger results by placing boys and girls at alternate desks along a row.

- **How far is a concern for relationships reflected in the curriculum?** Core curriculum subjects tend to emphasise individual activity and performance. Outside the core curriculum – in drama, PE and music – there's a greater emphasis on groups, providing an opportunity for children to internalise ideas like co-operation and fairness. So does the school offer 'softer' subjects like drama, where relational issues can come forward – or are these squeezed off the timetable? With this in mind, you could also ask if the school has any conscious policy about activities at break-time and after school. How much time does the school allocate to extra-curricular work? And to what extent does the school celebrate non-academic performance by pupils?

- **Is there a clear care structure within the school?** Children need someone to go to for help, advice, or a listening ear. Are staff available for this throughout the day, or is it pushed to the end of the afternoon when teachers are less pressured but more tired? Also, be aware that care structures don't always work. If you ask a child, 'Who do you go to if you have a problem?', does that child name the right person?

- **How strong are the school's links to the community?** Are visits made by clergy and community leaders? Also, there's the question of how the school relates to children's families. Is the Parent Teacher Association seen only as a fund-raising group, or as a means of engaging parental interest in the life and decision-making of the school? By what means does the school maintain an active relationship with parents and keep them informed?

A school leadership that's alert to the importance of relationships should have thought through the implications. In all of these areas, do you sense a consistent pattern of thought – or is policy ad hoc and poorly developed?

4. Think before sending children to a sixth form college

In many parts of the UK, so-called 'sixth form colleges' were instituted by the Thatcher government of the 1980s. Those students between the ages of 16 and 18 who wished to transfer to a sixth form college could be taught a broader range of subjects than was available in most secondary schools.

Academically, the sixth form college may make sense. In terms of relationships, though, it remains problematic. Students only stay there for two years – which produces a constant 'churning' of relationships. Also, the separation from lower years often has a negative impact both on the transferring students and on the schools they leave behind. The 16–18s are more likely to be sealed within their peer group, and deprived of formative responsibilities for younger members of the school. Meanwhile, younger pupils lose important role-models and the chance to observe, informally, the transition from adolescence into adulthood.

Whether to send a child to a sixth form college, then, is a relational decision as well as an academic one. Late adolescence is a crucial period developmentally. Sent to a sixth-form college, a teenager will take on more quickly some of the independent roles of adulthood. But long-term, the cost could well be a reduced sense of responsibility for others. It's worth weighing carefully.

5. Ask the right questions on parent-teacher evenings

When you ask a teacher, 'How is my child doing?' you'll probably be thinking first of how far ahead – or behind – the child is in maths, reading, or science. Concern about relationships usually comes some way down the list. There are two exceptions to this rule: bullying – which gets most parents' attention – and the desire to keep your children away from 'bad company', usually defined as disruptive youngsters with difficult backgrounds and at high risk of getting into drug abuse or petty crime.

These are all valid concerns, and a good school will address them. But relationships also play a huge role in your child's ordinary classroom experience. How are groups used to facilitate friendship and teamwork? Does the teacher have time to understand and tackle your child's particular difficulties? Is there proper discipline?

The life of the school class is full of relational opportunities. A shortage of computers in the classroom needn't be seen as a threat to the educational attainment of the children. It's also a chance to teach them the real-life arts of co-operation, sharing, project collaboration, and the management of joint assets.

Also, be concerned for the teacher whose task it is to care for your child. Relatively long holidays notwithstanding, teaching is a demanding and exhausting job – even when you have a pleasant class. It follows that the quality of the education children receive will depend indirectly on the support structures around the teacher. Teachers need the confidence and support of the head. And the head, at whose desk the buck stops, needs the support of peers and mentors outside the school.

This makes *your* relationship with the teacher an important one for your child's education. Showing obvious support – being encouraging, expressing appreciation – makes a difference to the teacher's self-confidence and job satisfaction. If you think your child has received an undeserved ticking-off, approaching the teacher with discretion and open-mindedness will be far more beneficial than instinctively jumping to your child's defence. In relationship terms, official complaints to the head teacher should be seen as a remedy of last resort.

6. Be part of the solution

If you're not satisfied with the way your children's school is handling and teaching relationships, do something about it.

The London school my own (David's) children go to is a good example here. Five years ago, it was an averagely unsuccessful Church of England primary beset with all the usual problems of its inner city location. This year it was awarded the status of Beacon School. It has one of the best disciplinary records in London. A recent OFSTED report – by the government body detailed to oversee educational standards – found virtually nothing to criticise. And it is delivering academic results in the top five per cent for the borough.

What drove the change? I think just two things. First, the appointment of a head teacher able to forge staff into an effective and dedicated team. And second, behind the head, a strongly-led board of governors with expertise in management, finance, education, and the Byzantine workings of the Local Education Authority.

This is not a school where teachers are left to do whatever teachers do. It is a school where a substantial number of parents have formed strong supportive relationships with staff. They give their professionalism and creative energy to the task of making the school a success. And they care about the children's social development as much as their academic performance.

Making yourself available to serve as a governor, then, is one way of bringing positive influence to bear on a school. But there are other ways too.

Schools have well-tried channels of communication. Parents' evenings give an opportunity to ask about relational issues. Alternatively, you can ask the Parent Teacher Association (PTA) to put on an evening that deals specifically with relationship issues. Or you can bring your concerns to the attention of teaching staff, head teacher, and governors. Most schools appreciate constructive engagement.

Almost certainly, the school's mission statement will contain paragraphs dealing with relationship issues. This is important, because it provides a standard against which to assess the practice of the school.

In the light of the mission statement, ask what part of the school curriculum and budget is being allocated to ensure that relationship issues are adequately addressed, and how individual teachers are turning the rhetoric into reality.

In the last analysis, the idea that we should teach our children to be independent is misguided. We teach our children independence, and then moan that they've 'grown away from us'. Of course children need the skills to hold their own and prosper in tomorrow's world. But the watchword is going to be *interdependence.* It's the children who learn the 'fourth R' – relationships – who will be best equipped to handle life in the next generation.

---

1   Michael Moynagh and Richard Worsley, *Using the future to understand the present* (London: Lexicon Editorial Services, 2000), p.58.
2   Valerie Bayliss, *Redefining Work* (London: RSA, 1998), p.51.
3   'At best, IQ contributes about 20 per cent to the factors that determine life success, which leaves 80 per cent to other forces ... My concern is with a key set of these 'other characteristics', emotional intelligence ... No one can yet say exactly how much of the variability from person to person in life's course it accounts for. But what data exist suggest it can be as powerful, and at times more powerful,

than IQ.' Daniel Goleman, *Emotional Intelligence: Why it can matter more than IQ,* (London: Bloomsbury, 1996), p.34.

4   See John Macmurray, *Persons in Relation* (London: Faber & Faber, 1961), pp.24 & 211.

5   For an able exposition of this point, see Michael Moynagh and Richard Worsley, *op.cit.*, pp.56–66.

6   The Centre for Economic Performance, August 1999. Bottom position was occupied by Portugal.

7   Reported verbally by an advisor to the Department for Education and Employment, 2000.

CHAPTER SIXTEEN

CITIES

Think of Paris. Almost certainly, you'll think first of buildings: the Eiffel Tower, Notre-Dame, L'Arc de Triomphe, Montmartre, Le Louvre.

But these architectural splendours are really a sort of by-product. What defines Paris – what lies behind and created its unmistakable skyline – springs from the kinds of relationships that link its citizens together. Relationships between individuals. Relationships between organisations. And relationships between generations.

A city's power to generate wealth naturally throws up a web of largely economic relationships that govern how wealth is moved around and used. Banks finance companies. Companies employ workers. Workers support the civic administration by paying tax. One generation leaves a legacy to the next in the form of art collections, architecture, gardens, and transport systems.

Wealth generation also has another effect. It sucks in new people – which is one reason why 60 per cent of the world's population will be living in cities by 2020.[1] And this, in turn, gives cities their peculiar relational flavour. For the further a city expands, the less likely it is that these remoter, economic relationships will be reinforced by personal ones.

In a smaller settlement, people's paths cross fairly frequently in local playgrounds, shops, and pubs. As a typical city-dweller, though, you'll probably know only a tiny percentage of your fellow citizens – and most of those will be people around your immediate neighbourhood or place of work. Furthermore, the composition of the city will constantly change as people slip in and out, a process facilitated in the West by the fact that you can plug into local services with little more than a letter or a phone call.

The problem of anonymity that results from this is endemic to large cities everywhere, and we will return to it in the chapter on strangers. For now, though, we want to point out that you can – if you want – find ways of re-energising the interpersonal, inter-organisational, and intergenerational relationships that can make a city a rewarding place to live.

INTERPERSONAL RELATIONSHIPS:
THE PROBLEM OF HAVES AND HAVE-NOTS

Cities, often more than nations, have been able to engage the pride and loyalty of local citizens. This has something to do with scale – you can, at least, see most of the city you live in from the nearest high ground. It's also true that some recent developments have strengthened the sense of civic unity. The soccer club, for example, in smaller cities like Bradford and Norwich. And local radio – especially since the advent of the mobile phone, which has increased participation by listeners and given them the added role of information source on traffic conditions.

At the same time, cities have always been divided. Lines of division are complex. American inner cities, particularly, have often turned into ethnic patchworks, with waves of foreign immigrants arriving in the centre and gradually melting into the periphery.

Comparable racial and religious divisions can be found in British cities. Many of London's past ghettoes are now enshrined in place names (Little Italy, Petty France). On the west coast of Britain, cities like Liverpool and Glasgow still have strong divisions between Protestants and Catholics.

More pervasive than all these, however, is the distinction between the haves and the have-nots. At an international level, poverty – often to the degree of utter destitution – is a safe distance away, and charities have to work hard to persuade you that the poor are 'your responsibility'. In the city, the reverse applies. The unemployed on the 'sink' estates, and the homeless on the streets, are your fellow citizens.

Not being in work, and not having a home, are very clearly relationships issues. No job means no money, and no money means no Christmas tree or family holiday, and no chance of buying a round of drinks for your friends. You get cut adrift, lose your sense of self-worth.

Signs of neglect in the city – graffiti, gratuitous damage to signs, rubbish left in public areas – usually indicate alienation between those who have money and those who don't. This distinction is often expressed in starkly spatial terms. Many British cities are divided geographically along the line of the prevailing wind – the wealthier suburbs lying to the west, where they were less likely to be affected by industrial smoke.

The effects of this on health standards are often striking. In Sheffield, the chances of dying before the age of 65 in the inner city are about one in seven. In the more affluent western parts, the chances are about one in twenty. In the United States different measures are used, but they tell the same story. In terms of potential life lost before the age of 75, residents of Washington DC, which has a large inner city population, lose three-and-a-half more years than residents of the more affluent Montgomery County, next to DC.[2]

In reality, a lot of money passes from richer to poorer zones in cities. For example, in the UK, taxpayers in a city subsidise the unemployed and low earners in their city through family credit and other benefits. But because this link goes via national government, it passes largely unseen, and fails to convey any sense that those who pay are concerned about those who benefit. Most cities do not possess financial mechanisms whereby wealthier citizens can address directly the poverty and unemployment of less fortunate fellow citizens.

In the worst cases, a large number of key relationships linking the unemployed to the economic core of the city – via schools, colleges, police and social services – all but break down. This lack of local connectedness results in the growth of no-go areas where even law enforcement becomes difficult, and where the imposition of security measures becomes yet another factor in alienation between haves and have-nots.

INTER-ORGANISATIONAL RELATIONSHIPS:
THE URBAN MATRIX

Relationships between organisations are influential because each organisation represents a large number of individual members. If two organisations relate badly, the city as a whole will suffer.

In some older British cities like Liverpool, for example, the relationship between the chamber of commerce and the city council has often been very poor. The city council has been controlled by traditional left-wing elements distrustful of employers. Consequently, in a time when traditional manufacturing industry has been in decline, there has been little co-operative discussion, and, as a result, little inward investment. The legacy is large-scale unemployment going back to the early 1980s.

Your city and its hinterland can be thought of as a matrix of relationships. Figure 2 shows a simplified version of this idea, with the city as a circle within which lines between the various constituent groups represent opportunities for relationships to develop – or not develop. At a local level, a hospital will thus have dealings with local government, and also with the companies from which it buys goods and services, local transport providers, and the charities that may fund areas of medical research.

Policing is another area where good inter-organisational relationships pay dividends. Effective policing depends heavily on co-operation between police forces and, for example, the community groups that are able to inculcate trust at street level and to deter burglary through informal surveillance. Similarly, the ability of police and schools to work together will affect the movement and use of illegal drugs in the city.

Of course, no organisation is monolithic. Large organisations relate through many different departments and at many different levels. Also, links between organisations often depend on links between particular individuals, and may break down when one of those individuals is promoted or transferred.

Nevertheless, new and creative ways can often be found of establishing linkages across the city. In one area of south Australia, for example, companies have come together with schools to ensure that no student ever leaves school without either going straight into a job or going for further education.

And within the UK, the Monsall Future Partnership, which brings together a local authority and three local housing associations in Manchester, has established a common set of standards and targets for the relationship between tenants and landlords. Tenants sign up to a Community Declaration, which commits them (among other things) to use reasonable language with neighbours and to keep balconies tidy. Landlords' responsibilities include removing offending graffiti within a week, and inspecting the area monthly with volunteer residents.

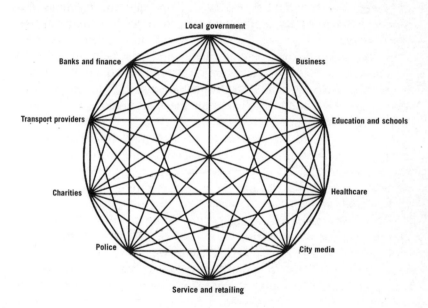

Figure 2 Inter-organisational relationships within a city

INTERGENERATIONAL RELATIONSHIPS: PLANTING FOR TOMORROW

Sir Winston Churchill once said, 'We shape our buildings, and after that they shape us.' Anyone who has lived on one of Britain's bleaker postwar council housing estates will know exactly what he was talking about. And in this case the irony is all the harsher because those who designed them were full of high hopes and good intentions.

All architecture is history. Every office block, public building, house, road, square and park has found a place in the city because citizens of a previous age decided it should be there. Each generation passes its urban hardware down to the next, and the next generation often has to live with the consequences. Thus today's motorists in the City of London squeeze their way around a street plan laid down centuries before the invention of the internal combustion engine.

On the positive side, we often owe a debt of thanks to past philanthropists and urban planners. Wealthy donors have planted parks and gardens and then given the land to the municipality. Impressive period architecture may now serve the public good as an art gallery or museum.

On the negative side, short-sighted industrial land-use in many European cities has left a legacy of derelict and polluted sites. Old factories have to be dismantled, and pollution has to be treated – often expensively – if we want to put the land back into service for housing or recreation.

And changes are still going on. The British pharmacist Boots recently announced plans to close 'a few dozen' smaller stores, and to focus instead on opening thirty larger, more profitable outlets in out-of-town locations The old 'High Street' stores were 'no longer commercially viable'.[3]

This widespread shift of British retailing to more distant, car-accessed locations has lasting consequences. A study, by the School of Architecture, Planning and Landscape at the UK's University of Newcastle-upon-Tyne, for example, revealed that two marginalised neighbourhoods had suffered a massive closure of local shops. And yet only 14 of the 40 households interviewed could use a car-based supermarket for their regular shopping.[4]

TAKING THE R OPTION IN CITIES

In St Andrews in Scotland, where I (David) lived for a number of years, the local newspaper has two names. The first, bestowed by some local cynics, is the Two-Minute Silence – two minutes being roughly the length of time needed to extract the week's news. The other name – its official one – is *The St Andrews Citizen*.

Photographs of public occasions framed in one of the local coffee houses suggest that the town once had a strong civic tradition. This hasn't entirely gone. But the lifting of administrative power from local to regional and national level – as well as an influx of newcomers attracted by the university and the golf course – has weakened the town's sense of itself as a coherent community.

Nevertheless, such a sense can still be found in larger settlements. In fact, civic pride – the feel-good factor as applied to your local urban area and its history and traditions – has come back into fashion. Glasgow isn't Barcelona, yet Glaswegians hold their city in some affection.

Translating a vague sense of belonging into real and constructive relationships (not just paying your tax to the city administration) is what we really mean by the term 'civic engagement'. To that extent, being rooted must involve *being rooted in a geographical area.*

You can carry your occupational pension from place to place easily enough. You can even carry relationships with family and friends. But the links that tie you into the civic networks of London or San Francisco are not the same ones that will tie you into the civic networks of Manchester or Miami. Local civic integration takes time to build up.

So how do you go about doing it?

1. Network your neighbours

Craig Newmark used to be the stereotypical geek: he even had glasses held together with Sellotape. Then when he moved to San Francisco, he got fed up with being lonely, and began emailing his few acquaintances about upcoming events on the city's arts scene. Six months later his 'list' had grown to 200, and soon 'Craig's List' became a kind of self-generating message board for Bay area surfers.

The list finally turned into a group-run non-profit organisation – 'an active source of support to the community...sponsoring training, mentoring, showcasing our community's talents, and giving other forms of help. We believe that the community members can help each other accomplish these changes, and we will facilitate those efforts.'[5]

This sort of interchange could develop naturally at the level of the immediate neighbourhood, which represents an underused resource for most of us. Neighbours can do things for one another that local services can't – like watering the garden or feeding the cat while you're on holiday. Also, many residential streets will house a staggering wealth of experience and technical expertise which could be tapped if only the individuals knew one another.

2. Work on key relationships within the city from your office desk

Your professional position may give you opportunities to bring organisations into greater contact and co-operation. Many of the key relationships in the city can be influenced strategically and profoundly by people working in the private and public sectors, as well as those in parts of the unregistered economy – like those working at home to bring up children.

Look for chances to help the interface between key organisations within the city. For example, between schools and the local university, between the police and schools, between the police and hospitals, between social services and the homeless. The benefits of this co-operation are multifaceted, including wealth creation, job creation, and better health outcomes. The British charity Common Purpose specialises in just this kind of linkage, bringing up-and-coming leaders in a city into contact with the movers and shakers in its various sectors.[7]

In the long run, this kind of 'joined-up' organisation in the city will tend to result in an increase in trust and commitment between its different communities, and, consequently, a lowering of crime rates. Stronger relationships in the city mean better overall morale, and a heightened sense of common purpose.

3. Spend and invest in your own city

The movement of money within the city influences levels of employment and the prosperity of local business. Directing money towards the areas that need it isn't just the business of national government – in fact, regional investment designed to boost employment may have little discernible effect in your particular city.

Targeted local investment, though, is a different thing. Recent tax proposals by the government in Britain offer tax credits to those who invest in inner city areas; groups like the Aston Reinvestment Trust in

Birmingham could become a target of much greater individual and corporate investment.

The charity City*life*, an offshoot from the Relationships Foundation, has also pioneered the idea of employment bonds – a financial instrument that allows wealthier citizens or ex-citizens to lend money for a five-year term for socially productive purposes. For example, the capital sum is used for social housing or workspace development, where the construction labour is drawn as far as possible from the local unemployed, and the interest, forgone by investors, goes directly into local job creation initiatives.

Originally piloted in Sheffield, where the scheme raised almost £1 million, employment bonds have now been implemented in Newcastle upon Tyne, East London and Portsmouth, with similar schemes pending in areas as diverse as Cornwall, Hull, Medway, Nottingham and Glasgow.[7]

Look out for opportunities like these for using your money to invest directly in your city. You way want also to give money to local charities that direct resources – human and financial – towards the disadvantaged in the city. Such schemes include, not just helping the unemployed, but benefiting the homeless and recycling urban waste.

It's also worth supporting local business. The prevalence of the word 'nearest' in online service locators like the UK's upmystreet.com inevitably encourages the making of local connections. And local shops and services – the places you probably still depend on for your late-night pint of milk or Sunday papers – only remain within reach if you make a point of using them.

The key role played by local retailers has been recognised by organisations like Community Enterprise Limited, which in the last five years has opened two community-owned convenience stores in the middle of Edinburgh's worst housing schemes. The shops have created jobs, shopping facilities and funds for the local communities.[8]

4. Lend your expertise

An urban community will contain thousands of highly skilled people – and also many organisations where those skills are desperately needed. But often the two do not connect.

Governing bodies in schools rely heavily on members who know about budgeting and have an inside track on national and local education policy. Bringing such competences to a school can make the difference between success and failure for the entire institution. Similar crucial opportunities exist in public enquiries, planning enquiries, community health councils, local charities, and sports clubs.

The skills don't always have to be sophisticated. A group in Edinburgh called Positive Help sends volunteers to assist people who have HIV/AIDS with ordinary tasks like shopping, painting and wall-papering.[9] Such cross-cutting relationships have particular value in the city, because they often bridge the gap between the west end and the east end, the haves and have-nots.

Benefit also passes the other way. For example, less affluent areas will often make a substantial impact on a city's cultural life – as is the case with London's Notting Hill Carnival, and many of the UK's major football clubs.

5. Take local democracy seriously

It's easy to be cynical about local politics. Councillors are often dismissed as people either not clever enough to stand for the local parliamentary seat, or self-important hotshots for whom local office is a leg up to the 'real thing'. In addition, there's the bother of making yet another tiresome visit to the polling station when you really ought to be fixing the car. And, of course, we all have that nagging feeling, even when General Elections roll around, that our vote doesn't count for much anyway.

The fact remains, though, that local politics, with all its flaws, is the mechanism by which you exert your influence over policy-making at the city level. As George W. Bush discovered in 2000, very small numbers of votes can sometimes swing very big elections. The same is true for city and local administrations. Often only 30 per cent of the electorate turn out for local elections in the UK.

True, centralisation of power has undermined local government by removing many of its powers – particularly the power to raise taxes – and government ministers can sometimes overrule local decisions.

But that doesn't make voting in local elections an insignificant act. It gives you an excuse to find out what the local issues are, and what the candidates have to say about them. And it gives you relational opportunities – like joining a political party and showing your concern for your city by attending meetings and putting forward your point of view.

---

1   According to the Population Institute in Washington, DC. Notably, however, 34% of those living in a big city in the UK have a yearning for the country life – a feeling not reciprocated by country-dwellers, less than 5% of whom relish moving to a big city. Around three-quarters (72%) of those living in a country village want to stay put, compared with only 30% of those living in a big city. Source: Roger Jowell, John Curtice, Alison Park, Katarina Thomson, Lindsey Jarvis, Catherine Bromley and Nina Stratford (eds.), *British Social Attitudes* (London: Sage, 2000).
2   Data for Sheffield from the Office for National Statistics, Annual District Death Extracts, 1996–1998. Data for Washington DC from East Carolina University's Center for Health Services Research and Development.
3   *European Retail*, October 2000, Issue 254.
4   S. Speak & S. Graham, *Service not Included: the social implications of private service restructuring in marginalised neighbourhoods* (Bristol: Policy Press, 2000).
5   Reported in *R Briefing*, Issue 23. Available from the Relationships Foundation. Craig's list can be found at: http://www.craigslist.org
6   For information on Common Purpose, see:
    http://www.commonpurpose.org.uk/home.vdf
7   For further information, visit the Citylife website:
    www.relationshipsfoundation.org/citylife/Index.html
8   See the full case study at: www.celltd.demon.co.uk/study.htm
9   This organisation was set up through the Episcopal Church of Scotland, and can be contacted via the church office in Edinburgh.

CHAPTER SEVENTEEN

SECURITY

I (David) once lived in an old tenement accessed by a narrow spiral staircase. Not knowing many other people who lived on the same stair, I didn't think twice one afternoon when I passed a man coming down with a camera in his hand. Only when I got to the fourth floor and found my front door kicked open and my drawers pulled out did it occur to me that it was *my* camera he'd been carrying out.

The crime was not particularly serious, as crimes go. Nevertheless, I remember feeling two things very strongly. The first was a righteously angry thirst for revenge (kicking the thief down the staircase would have done nicely).

The second was powerlessness. For I never saw the thief again, and although the police obligingly sent around a fingerprint expert, it was clear that one smudge on a door handle wasn't going to win me the redress I desired. And I hadn't even insured the camera.

But if the thief had been apprehended, I still doubt if the outcome would have been very satisfactory.

Under English law, a person who steals your camera (or, for that matter, rapes you or attacks you with a machete) is not considered to be perpetrating an act against *you*. The offence is against the *state.* From the moment you report the crime, it becomes the business of the police and the courts to catch the offender, secure a conviction, and administer the punishment.

This system was started under King John, with sound intentions. When a crime was committed, the state stepped in to represent the victim, first to ensure that justice was done, and second to discourage the victim from taking the law into his or her own hands.

In practice, however, the state's intervention has often resulted in the victim and the victim's relatives being largely excluded from the process. Though the judge may take into account the crime's impact on them when passing sentence, they have no direct say in sentencing. And experience shows that even the satisfaction of seeing the offender put away for a reasonable period does not undo the personal affront of crime or the emotional damage it leaves behind.

WHY CRIME IS A RELATIONSHIP PROBLEM

Crime *only* happens in a relationship. In many cases, the relationship already has a history. In both the USA and the UK, 60 per cent of violent crimes involve people who already know each other.[1] But even if no relationship existed before, crime instantly creates one.

This doesn't require you to have met the offender face-to-face. Come back to find your flat turned over, and you'll see just how effectively your life and the offender's have been stuck together. As one researcher put it, 'whether or not they ever meet, the offender and the victim are locked into a relationship. Without knowing each other in reality, they know each other intimately in their imaginations.'[2]

The anger you feel is anger against the *offender*. The hurt and vulnerability you feel is focused on what the *offender* has done to you. And the uncertainty and anxiety with which you look to the future are tied up closely with what the *offender* may be doing.

By their nature, broken relationships leave us wanting resolution. We feel uncomfortable with loose ends. We want to tie things up and move on. It's not easy to close an emotional door on the mess by simple dint of will. And it's particularly hard if, as is often the case, the police do not trace the offender or secure a conviction, and the offender is 'still out there'.

An offence, then, should be seen not as an abstract violation of laws, but as a wrong committed by one human being against another. It's an existing relationship turning sour, or a new and unwelcome one suddenly springing up. And regardless of what does or doesn't happen in the courts, this relationship remains at the heart of the issue.

In passing, it's worth noting also that a crime drags in more than one relationship. There are also secondary victims. The child who is traumatised by a burglary next door. Or the older lady who hears of a local mugging and is then afraid to walk to the shops. It doesn't help to insist that the real risk is small. It's the perceived risk that disturbs people's peace of mind, changes their behaviour and gives them nightmares.

CRIMINAL BEHAVIOUR IS NOT THE NORM

But take a step back. A key starting point in dealing with crime – whether or not you've already been on the receiving end – is to see those who commit offences as *people*. We don't do anyone any favours – least of all ourselves – by stereotyping criminals as monsters.

For one thing, the large majority of criminals are socially dysfunctional – damaged individuals from damaged home backgrounds. None of which excuses their behaviour. But it does put offenders as a group in a different category from, say, vampires.

The person who stole my camera was not a worthless rogue. He was a person like me, with needs like mine, who'd lost the plot when it comes to living a purposeful and productive life.

As one down-to-earth judge put it recently:

> *Most criminals are very inadequate. Of course, they are criminals and should be punished, but, day in day out, people come to court partly because of their own inadequacy, often after the most wretched start in life. Violence in the family, sexual abuse, separation of parents (if they had a relationship with their father at all), frequent changes of home, very little money and an inability to handle what money there is – the list is endless ... whatever the press and public may say, they should be helped as well as punished.*[3]

Most of us can just about see this when the offenders are young. One of the most respected studies of delinquent boys, tracked over a period of twenty years, identified their defining characteristics in the following way:

- They were from low-income families.
- They were from large families with a criminal parent.

- They were from families that exercised poor supervision of children.

- They were often of low intelligence and troublesome at school.[4]

John Harding, when he was Chief Probation Officer for the Inner London Probation Service, argued that government directives to be 'tough on crime' – largely driven by public opinion – make the problem worse. He had to deal first-hand with the 'sad, chaotic and blighted lives' of young offenders.[5]

True, poverty doesn't help. True, some forms of criminality – like paedophilia – have psychiatric roots. And true, the older a person gets, the more effectively he or she will suppress the pain. But the average British jail is populated, in the main, not by irredeemable 'hard cases', but by grown-ups who have never been able to resolve the misery, hurt and misdirection they suffered as children.

Harding quotes a letter sent to him by a man who'd been kept in residential care and prisons for over thirty years:

> *All my life it seems I've been running but all I ever wanted was to belong somewhere and yet I've never found it...Deep down I'm a lonely person and the loneliest place I know is prison.*[6]

We are labouring this point a little because our collective fear of crime – of being mugged, raped, or burgled – tends to distort our view. Ordinary people like you and me are made to feel weak and vulnerable, when in fact it is the criminal who has lost his way and needs help.

TAKING THE R OPTION IN SECURITY

Crime affects you in two ways. First, it increases your tax bill. Crime in England and Wales costs the taxpayer a stunning £60 billion a year – more than the total spent on defending and running the country.[7] Parallel figures for the USA are, in the words of the *New York Times,* 'eye-popping'. The 49 million crimes committed annually in the USA cost: $345 billion each year in pain, suffering, and reduced quality of life; $105 billion each year in medical bills and lost earnings; $45 billion each year in compensation to crime victims from insurers; and

$40 billion each year to run the nation's prisons, jails and parole and probation systems.[8]

Second, though, crime creates relationships in which you may be the target. Petty theft is so common that Americans have a 99 per cent chance of being affected by it.[9] In many Western countries, however, there's also a perception – fortified by intense media coverage of incidents like child killings – that public space has become a high-risk area. We don't feel safe alone at night. We don't let young children go to school unaccompanied.

One response is to arm yourself. A soccer fan who supported Liverpool Football Club in the 1960s told me (David) recently how he would sew razor blades under the lapels of his coat in case a supporter of an opposing team should try to grab hold of him. But strategies designed to help beat off an attacker – martial arts, carrying weapons – don't really get to the root of the problem. If you want to protect yourself and those you love, it's not the flash-points themselves you most need to worry about. It's the conditions causing those flash-points to occur.

1. Get your parenting right

It's just a fact that young people sometimes do stupid things. And sometimes those stupid things get them into trouble with the law.

By the age of 30, one in three young men in Britain have been convicted by a court.[10] The peak age for male offending is 18, and for female, 15. Less than a fifth of those cautioned return to the attention of the police within two years. The vast majority of young offenders, in other words, are temporary offenders. It's a phase they grow out of.

The key issue, really, is not whether your child gets into trouble, but whether he or she is able to put these learning experiences aside and move forward.

Good communication between parents and teenagers plays a significant role here. If you can spend time with your children, you will know what challenges they're facing and keep the lines open for them to ask for help and advice. You don't have to be a genius or a saint. You just have to be available, honest and ready to accept them. That's one of the main levers available to parents in keeping their children from abusing alcohol, experimenting with drugs, or driving dangerously.

2. Use community networks

It's no longer possible – if it ever was – to rely on the police for local security. No quantity of police on the beat will eradicate crime – a fact most police forces acknowledge. If you want to put an effective curb on criminal activity in your local area, you need to mobilise the network of local interests. People who live or work in the area, know the scene, know the problems, and are motivated to do something about it.

The classic expression of this is the neighbourhood watch scheme. These are not – as is often thought – relays of old ladies peeking out of net curtains. The really effective schemes bring together large numbers of people, and plug into whatever relevant agency resources are available. They target local crimes and devise ways of preventing them.

All that's needed is a number of neighbours willing to form a com-mittee and come up with specific proposals, which can be imple-mented with the assistance of the local council or the police. Neighbourhood watch has 160,000 groups covering five million households. With a little initiative, serious resources can be brought to bear. And, of course, there's the added benefit that social barriers are broken down.

In a neighbourhood of Newcastle in the UK, a community-run security project was set up by local residents, including the police, the vicar and local housing officers. They took over an empty tower block apartment as a control room. Those in the control room act as concierge for the block and organise patrols of the surrounding area. The project manager reports a drop of more than 50 per cent in reported local crime. Vandalism has been reduced, employment has been provided, and the number of empty properties reduced.[11]

3. Exercise control in your relationships

If you're cornered in a dark alley by three Mafia hit men, your options are probably limited. But many potential crime situations give you much more chance to exercise forethought and caution. You can't easily influence another person's passions or criminal intent. But there are ways of managing the situation that help to prevent an offence taking place. For example:

- **Stay in control of your faculties** If you overdose on alcohol, you incapacitate yourself. You put yourself at higher risk of having a driving accident, having your property stolen, or being raped. You're not 'asking for it' in the sense of deserving to be taken advantage of simply because you're over the limit. You're just weakening your defences.

- **Don't allow yourself to be isolated** As far as possible, travel with people you know. And when you are forced to travel on your own, keep some means of establishing contact with others – a mobile phone or personal alarm.

- **Don't role-play the victim in advance** Studies show that violent offenders will often select people who look like 'easy targets'. For example, a person who walks with a slouch and appears to have low self-esteem is more likely to be attacked than a person who walks erect and with a bold, strong stride.

- **Establish eye contact early on** This pre-empts the possibility of being surprised, and increases your chances of being able to identify a suspect if an offence occurs – a strong disincentive to most would-be attackers.

4. When possible, make a criminal face up to relationships

Someone once told me (Michael) about a burglar with a particularly bad conscience. He was so ashamed of the hurt he was causing that, before he could begin a burglary, he had to turn around all the family pictures on the mantelpiece.

Shame is a powerful deterrent. Yet one of many problems associated with prosecution by the state is that offenders are shielded from the human consequences of their actions. Because they never have to confront the victim as a person, they can far more easily retreat into mind games that justify their actions. 'He's rich – he won't miss what I took.' Or, 'She's insured.' Or, 'We were only having fun.'

This is a form of ego-protection that's only too easy to maintain from the safe seclusion of a prison. And, of course, it lays the psychological foundations for further offending after the prisoner has been released. Partly for this reason, a new way of resolving the damage done in the victim/offender relationship is increasingly being used – the procedure of mediation.

With the agreement of both sides, and with a qualified mediator in charge, some form of communication is set up between the offender and the person he or she has wronged. Each case of mediation is different, and outcomes vary depending on the individuals involved. Ideally, the mediator will aim to set up a face-to-face meeting, which can have striking benefits for both parties:

> *A woman and her eight-year-old son were the victims of an aggravated burglary, in which they were terrorised by the burglar. He received a prison sentence. The boy's nightmares persisted and as time drew near for the burglar to be released the woman became apprehensive that the burglar would return. She approached her local advice centre, who referred her to the local Mediation and Reparation Service.*
>
> *The mediators visited the offender who had just been released. He was upset to hear that his victim was still so worried. A meeting was arranged at the advice centre, at which the offender apologised in full and reassured the victim that he had no intention of returning to cause harm. The victim accepted the apology and reassurance, and said that she found the meeting helpful. The boy's nightmares stopped soon afterwards.[12]*

Mediation cases often involve reparation – the offender doing something to put right the wrong. A mid-1980s study by the British Home Office showed that agreement was reached in 80 per cent of mediation cases, and that face-to-face meetings, particularly, had a positive effect on re-offending rates.[13]

Clearly such meetings need skilled handling and aren't always appropriate – for example, in cases of rape. But often, for the person affected by the crime, they can resolve the personal issues far more effectively than a court judgement.

They can also break powerfully into the closed circle of self-justification used by the offender. For offenders who have known only rejection and hardship, being *forgiven* by the person they've harmed can be deeply affecting, and open up new possibilities for trust.

5. Help to change the climate

From a relationships viewpoint, imprisonment is about the worst way of tackling crime. In many cases, you remove the criminal from the only supportive relationships he or she has – with family and friends – and instead place him or her in a community made up entirely of other offenders. After release, many return to find what relationships they had now lying in ruins, and cannot get employment because of their criminal record. Not surprisingly, in the UK about 53 per cent re-offend within two years.[14]

One idea you might consider in the R option for security, then, is doing something to help an offender find a route back into mainstream society. There are many ways of countering the social exclusion of imprisonment. You can become a prison visitor, join the Board of Visitors in a prison, start a correspondence with a prisoner. If you run a company, consider giving an ex-offender a job. A project like this in effect puts crime into reverse. Instead of the offender impacting on you, you impact on the offender.

Fr. Peter Young, a 70-year-old Catholic priest, has been working with offenders in Albany, New York, for 33 years. Go into the Schuyler Inn Young set up and you'll find it staffed entirely by ex-prisoners. General manager Oscar Peterson spent twenty-five years behind bars and was, by his own admission, 'an addictive and habitual criminal'. Today he's in charge of a large staff and will tell you, 'Now I give people hope. They look at me and say, there is a new way.'[15]

You don't think you could do something like that? Maybe it's not such a dumb idea to try.

1   US Census Bureau, *Statistical Abstract of the United States:2000,* No.342. The 2000 British Crime Survey England and Wales (available on http://www.homeoffice.gov.uk/rds/pdfs/hosb1800.pdf).

2   T. Marshall & S. Merry, *Crime and Accountability: Victim/Offender Mediation in Practice* (London: HMSO, 1990), p.1.

3   Christopher Compston, 'Local Justice: A Personal View,' in Jonathan Burnside and Nicola Baker (eds), *Relational Justice: Repairing the Breach* (Winchester: Waterside Press, 1994), p.89.

4   D. West & D. Farrington, *Delinquency, its Roots and Careers* (Cambridge, 1977). Since published in a book: D. West, *Delinquency: Its Roots, Careers and Prospects* (London: Heinemann, 1982), pp.29–30. Reprinted (Aldershot: Gower, 1986).

5 John Harding, 'Youth Crime: A Relational Perspective,' in Burnside & Baker (eds), *op.cit.*, p.105.

6 *Ibid.*

7 Home Office study, quoted in *The Times*, 23 December 2000.

8 Report from National Institute of Justice, quoted by National Centre for Policy Analysis, 1996.

9 The 2000 National Crime Prevention Survey. See:
   http://www.ncpc.org/rwesafe.htm

10 Home Office Statistical Bulletin 7/85, 'Criminal Careers of those born in 1953, 1958 and 1963' (Home Office: 1985).

11 Katherine Mumford, 'Home Sweet Home?' in *Relational Justice Bulletin,* Issue 5, January 2000. (Cambridge: Relationships Foundation). Past copies of the *Relational Justice Bulletin* can be downloaded from the Relationships Foundation's website at:
   www.relationshipsfoundation.org/relational_justice/RJ_bulletin_archives.html

12 Nicola Baker, 'Mediation, Reparation and Justice,' in Burnside & Baker, (eds), *op.cit.*, p.71.

13 T. Marshall & S. Merry, *op.cit.* Some schemes bring in not just victims but members of the offender's community. This system of community justice, developed from the one used traditionally in New Zealand's Maori communities, shames the offender far more powerfully than trial by a remote legal authority.

14 Richard Ford, 'Crime-busting tactics fail to reduce offences,' *The Times,* 22 July 2000.

15 See Penelope Lee, 'Happy Landings', *Relational Justice Bulletin, Issue 8,* pp.4–5, October 2000. (Cambridge: Relationships Foundation). See note 11 above.

CHAPTER EIGHTEEN

STRANGERS

In the winter of 1980, my wife and I (Michael) visited Delhi's Red Fort. It was a bad baby day. Our toddler was bawling, and a group of tourists sitting behind us on the bus, who'd decided he was bawling because he was cold, had begun to lecture my wife on the folly of bringing a small child out in this temperature without a hat.

In fact, you could no more put a hat on this particular child than you could put a saddle on a wild horse. But the Americans would not believe it, and the matter was only resolved when – to our astonishment – a hefty-looking punk intervened. Depositing himself in the seat opposite, he said, 'If these people give you any more trouble, you just let me know and I'll deal with them.'

The incident captures neatly the 'information problem' raised in dealings with a stranger. Live in Britain today, and you're likely to meet more people in one day than most medievals met in a lifetime. And that means you need a way of choosing – almost instantaneously – who you're going to trust. Otherwise, every encounter begins with a questionnaire.

Accordingly, we've grown quite skilled in the nuances of non-verbal communication. Clothing, hairstyle, facial expression, posture, age: all these things broadcast introductory signals about who we are and how we're likely to respond when approached.

But, of course, they *don't* tell us many of the things we most need to know. The punk on our Delhi trip (remember this was 1980) looked like he'd eat people alive – but he declared himself an ally. The old ladies who made up the tour party looked like pussycats – but they were tough as nails. In other words, although we depend heavily on this visual information, we're often misled. Strangers can surprise us.

'OPENING THE BOX'

On balance, we suspect, the surprise is likely to be pleasant, if only because we have a habit of assuming the worst. Our stereotypes often have a negative slant. We're too apt to dismiss another person as a 'typical accountant', a 'typical thug', or a 'typical black'. We look at the packaging, and never open the box to see what's inside. And this is a pity, because the boxes are a good deal less interesting than the things they contain.

It's a strong theme in national British culture to be reluctant to open up to strangers. Usually, something has to go seriously wrong before our natural reserve breaks down and we start to interact. Only in the presence of an overwhelming common cause – floods, a blizzard, Christmas, the Blitz – are we ready to put away our fear of seeming forward or of being drawn into an unseen trap.

The other day, I (Michael) travelled back from a remote corner of Britain on a railway system reduced to a near standstill by emergency rail inspections. What struck me wasn't the time it took to get home, but that complete strangers found something to say to one another. It began with general complaints and jokes about the railways, but it soon led to more serious conversation and even to offers of help.

Probably, in the vast majority of cases, strangers are good value for money once you get to know them. It's just that we don't usually bother.

SOLVE THE PROBLEM OF ENTANGLEMENT

In the early 1990s, a TV documentary team in Britain hired an actress to collapse in a busy street, and filmed the consequences. When they did this in a village, it took a minute and a half for the first person to stop and help. When they did it in an urban shopping mall, nobody stopped for *45 minutes*.[1]

The reasons for this 'not wanting to get involved' are complex. Underlying them, however, is a single and very simple idea. Like it or not, we're all equipped with a sense of responsibility for others. It's like a kind of gravitational pull. Smaller, less mobile communities multiply this force because inhabitants tend to have high rates of interaction. But the force is active everywhere. You don't have to be around another person for very long before you feel that he or she has some kind of claim on your goodwill.

Visiting Cairo, I (David) remember a perfume vendor ushering me into his premises and sitting me down for a cup of sugary Egyptian tea. The moment I stepped over the threshold, I knew I was going to have to buy something. His hospitality put me in his debt – which, no doubt, and with all due respect to Egyptian retailing, was part of the sales technique.

Emergencies have a similar effect. When you see someone lying in the street, you must either steel yourself and walk on by, or give in to that gravitational tug of conscience – and stop to help.[2]

You hesitate in these situations because 'involvement' carries a cost. You may have to part with money. You will certainly have to part with time. There is a danger you may be made to look foolish. Outside the circle of your immediate and close relationships, it doesn't take much, therefore, to convince you that another person poses some sort of threat – even lying on the pavement. Staying aloof seems the safer option, since it allows you to disregard the fact that, like you, the stranger is a person, with friends, relatives, and a point of view.

This has important pay-offs:

- **Avoiding entanglement allows you to use stereotypes** Suppose that you found out a certain person on your street had served ten years for a serious assault. You can't pretend this information wouldn't affect you – even if you had no evidence whatever to prove he or she was a current threat. Our attitude to a wide variety of individuals (football supporters, lager-drinking males, members of other ethnic groups, paedophiles, travellers) will be influenced by the anecdotes and news reports we've heard about the groups they represent. Nobody likes to think of himself as prejudiced. Nevertheless it can be hard to shake off the expectation that a member of this or that minority will be 'typically' violent, lazy, incompetent, untrustworthy, or hostile. And in the really important decisions – where we live, where we send our children to school – our attitudes will show.

- **Avoiding entanglement lets you regard misfortune as somebody else's problem** One of the most revealing and most uncomfortable experiences we have with the stranger happens when we come face to face with poverty. Recalling the elderly people on his street in North London, the philosopher Michael Ignatieff comments, 'They are dependent on the state, not upon me, and we are both glad of it. Yet I am also aware of how this mediation walls us off from each other. We are responsible for each other, but we are not responsible to each other.'³ The discomfort gets worse when the state has faded from the picture, and there is nothing left between you and the young person hunched in a doorway with his paper cup of coins. Nine times out of ten, we will avoid even making eye contact.

- **Avoiding entanglement lets you put yourself first** Much of our interaction with strangers is competitive – that is, geared to winning. Get stuck at a busy junction and – I promise – it won't be long before you think what an idiot the other driver is for marooning himself in the yellow box and blocking your way. Or consider your attitude to the person who somehow slips ahead of you in that mile-long queue at the airport check-in. A similar dynamic underlies public resentment of 'bogus asylum seekers' – either through increased pressure on availability of low-income housing, or, less directly, through the perception that abuse of the asylum system will one day make itself felt in taxes.

As a self-preservation measure, staying aloof has something to be said for it. You are only capable of sustaining so many close relationships, and clearly you can't treat every Tom, Dick or Harry you come across as if he, or she, were an intimate friend.

At the same time, you will recognise that aloofness carries its own cost. It doesn't fill you with pride to think that a woman can lie in the street, clearly needing help, yet be disregarded for the best part of an hour. You don't enjoy aggressiveness on the road. And you feel genuine concern for a young person sleeping rough, even if you can't bring yourself to do anything.

In short, stranger-relationships are apt to leave us with an uneasy conscience and a learned habit of suppressing empathetic feeling. It's a long way from the compassionate society we say we'd like to live in.

TAKING THE R OPTION WITH STRANGERS

Former New York mayor Rudolph Giuliani once attempted to reform the famously abusive manners of New Yorkers by asking them to turn their stereos down and say thank-you. This initiative wasn't helped much by Giuliani's own explosive temperament. But he was on the right track. If you want to create more rewarding and more effective relationships with people you don't know, you will need to translate that desire into positive action.

On the one hand, this is open to the objection that 'there's no point in me doing it if nobody else does'. On the other hand, societies everywhere are only an aggregate of individuals, who ultimately carry the can for sustaining decent social norms. Plus, there is a pay-off. It's trite but true that the satisfaction you get in your own experience of strangers will depend in part on your own attitude.

On 20 April, 1999, two Colorado high school students, Eric Harris and Dylan Klebold, attempted to blow up their school and its 450 pupils by placing propane bombs in the cafeteria. The bombs failed to explode. But Harris and Klebold managed to dispatch thirteen classmates with handguns before committing suicide.

The final note left on Eric Harris's computer is revealing:

By now, it's over. If you are reading this, my mission is complete...Your children who have ridiculed me, who have chosen not to accept me, who have treated me like I am not worth their time are dead...

Surely you will try to blame it on the clothes I wear, the music I listen to, or the way I choose to present myself, but no. Do not hide behind my choices. You need to face the fact that this comes as a result of YOUR CHOICES.

Parents and teachers...You have taught these kids to not accept what is different. YOU ARE IN THE WRONG. I have taken their lives and my own – but it was your doing.[4]

How two teenagers could resort to such an extreme action is a complex and important question. But the psychology behind it is familiar. Rightly or wrongly, Harris and Klebold felt themselves to be victims. They felt walled-in by other people's prejudice and insensitivity.

The point is: the way we treat strangers *does matter*. The kind of communities we want to live in are ones where people are included, not ostracised. The test isn't how we treat our friends, but how we treat the people on the fringes of our universe.

So here are some proposals:

1. Welcome strangers

One thing that's worth considering is how effectively you ease others into your own social group. This is all about the creation of relationships. Many schools will help a new student integrate by assigning him or her a 'buddy' – another student whose job it is to act as host, contact point, and source of information. The chair at a meeting will formally introduce the visitor. The host or hostess at the cocktail party will attach the new arrival to a conversational group, dropping a compliment or two as a way of giving the newcomer a profile.

Nuances are important. There are matters of etiquette (for example, do you introduce Michael Jackson to Prime Minister Blair, or Prime Minister Blair to Michael Jackson?). Also, you don't want to communicate the feeling that the visitor is being consumed by the group – as though he or she mattered only as a boost to attendance figures or as an addition to the mailing list.

Being a stranger – that is, without supportive relationships – in a meeting, in a company, or in a country, creates vulnerability. The stranger has no 'place'. And for that reason, people in this position appreciate hugely any effort others make to include them and make them feel valued.

This is particularly true of long-term strangers – of whom there are many in the academic community in Cambridge, where I (Michael) live. So if your company has transferred personnel from overseas, it's worth asking how open your home and family are, in the sense of being ready to extend informal hospitality. In India, the custom of children calling houseguests Uncle or Auntie does much to break the ice and produce a sense of acceptance. Perhaps we need some similar conventions in Western society.

2. Take the initiative

Moving through public space is an opportunity. The hundreds of other people with whom you share train carriages and airport lounges can

– if you bother to talk to them – provide you with fresh and interesting information and useful chance contacts.

On one occasion, I (Michael) had just stepped off a flight from Nairobi and was standing, bleary-eyed at 5.30 am, waiting for my luggage to come round on the carousel at Gatwick Airport. I noticed that the person standing next to me had luggage with a Cambridge label on it, and decided to ask him if he was going back there. He said he was.

I soon discovered that Dr Belbin runs a company assessing team-building relationships in corporates. He and his wife were extremely friendly, and offered me a lift back to Cambridge. This not only saved me a lot of time and trouble, but provided the opportunity to learn a great deal about relationship processes in team building.

Life – not just art – is full of chance encounters. Significant and productive relationships, including some notable romances, would never have got off the starting blocks if two people had not been stranded on the same station.

Even the humble potato owes a debt of gratitude to a chance meeting. When the young Dr John Niederhauser bumped into the Soviet genetic scientist Professor Nikolai Vavilov in a Moscow park in 1935, the meeting produced a solution to one of the crop's most serious blights.[5]

With a precedent like that, who can afford not to start a conversation?

3. Use courtesy to counter stress

The world is such that we deal with strangers regularly in stressed situations. Driving is a good example. According to US Government estimates, aggressive driving is responsible for a third of car crashes and two-thirds of the 42,000 annual road deaths in the United States.[6]

Aloofness is a common culprit here. Clearly, you wouldn't let your frustration out by leaning on your horn or yelling if you thought another driver would recognise you. Sharing the road with people you're never likely to see twice goes a long way to explaining why you're tempted to take the liberties you do.

It's dull to say it, but the discipline of courtesy is one of the most effective palliatives here. You have a relationship with other road users, other people in your office, other residents of the same street.

Make it a rule to practise courtesy, and you'll probably produce better outcomes all round.

4. Develop local contacts

Another question to ask is, Where do you do your shopping? Car-based superstores and retail parks have their place, but they do not offer the opportunity to turn staff from strangers into acquaintances.

Patronising your local corner store (if it still exists), or local pub, or local paper shop, fills your surrounding public space with real relationships. It also has the effect – indirectly – of building the social capital of the area, in the sense that you strengthen the network of local contact and local loyalty. A shopkeeper you know personally is also more likely to let you take your newspaper even if you've forgotten to bring any change.

5. Make someone's day

To what extent do you impact on the society you move through? Are you simply a consumer of goods and services – someone dominated and motivated by a fear of getting entangled with others? Or do you use your daily encounters with other people to do something constructive?

There's a longstanding tradition in the UK of being surly with functionaries. We treat certain classes of individual (parking attendants are a good example) as being almost deserving of our disdain. But bank clerks, telephone call centre staff, and even parking attendants are human beings with their own daily problems and difficulties. You bring pleasure and relief into their lives by acknowledging them. And in return – since they're only human – they will usually be more responsive and helpful to you.

At risk of seeming completely patronising, let us bring things to the simplest possible conclusion and say it's okay to make eye contact and smile. The smile communicates acceptance. It creates confidence. You want to do something for the homeless teenager on the street? Then look at him. Say something. The homeless people we've talked to say that human contact is worth a whole handful of coins. And it doesn't cost you a penny.

1   In the USA, there would be a reason for this – since anyone attempting to assist an accident victim might later be sued if his efforts could be shown to have worsened the victim's condition.

2   The story of the Good Samaritan is psychologically accurate, and suggests that little has changed in two thousand years.

3   Michael Ignatieff, *The Needs of Strangers* (London: Chatto & Windus, 1984), p.10.

4   See Dan Savage, 'Fear the Geek: Littleton's silver lining', The Stranger.com, Vol.8, no.33, 6–12 May 1999, at: http://www.thestranger.com/1999-05-06/feature2.html

5   The two co-operated in finding a genetic solution to potato blight. Recounted by Elmer E. Ewing, 'A chance encounter between an American Boy and a Russian Professor becomes impetus for global battle against blight' (speech at the World Potato Congress in June 2000).

6   Ian Brodie, 'Foul-mouthed Americans don't have a nice day,' *The Times*, 30 March 1998.

CHAPTER NINETEEN

EVERYTHING

People differ in the amount of emphasis they give to relationships. Nevertheless, our relationships – with friends, family, and colleagues, as well as those more distant ones that govern our political and financial affairs – exercise an enormous influence over the way we live and the quality of our living.

What we've called 'taking the R option' springs from the single idea that we benefit – individually and corporately – if we pay some serious attention to the way the world connects us together. The action-points we've put forward in previous chapters show that five issues with relationships are particularly important.

RECOGNISING THE RELATIONAL DIMENSION

In some situations, we forget that quality of relationship makes a crucial difference. This is particularly the case with health, cities, crime, schooling, and money.

Take a transaction I (David) witnessed recently in an electrical store. A customer was abusing a sales clerk because the camera she'd received for Christmas came with only a German-language instruction manual. Not a great matter. Yet the customer seemed unable to employ her relationship with the sales clerk to resolve the problem with efficiency and good humour. All she seemed to see was, on one side, the culpable negligence of the manufacturer, and, on the other, the monstrous affront she was being forced to bear as a consumer. Not surprisingly, this approach resulted in considerable delay and bad feeling all round.

MAKING ROOM FOR RELATIONSHIPS

This is not a call to ease back on work to 'make more time for your family', although it may involve that. It's the idea that relationships everywhere – in work and outside of work – need some thought, time and attention, and are the proper subject of scrutiny and setting of priorities. The chapter on management unpacked this, and showed how it involves things like seeing the other person often enough, spending enough time with that person, and meeting that person in different situations.

It also applies particularly in time management, and in the use of communications technology, which tends to increase the number of our contacts but decrease their depth.

DEVELOPING LONG-TERMISM

In the twenty-first century, we take for granted our freedom to withdraw from relationships at relatively short notice. The commercial world is dominated by short-term contracts, the personal world by an expectation that friendships and child-raising partnerships will not necessarily be for life. This has some advantages set against an alternative of rigidly enforced, and sometimes inappropriate, lifelong commitments.

But it also creates a problem. Many of the benefits that good relating delivers to business and personal life – benefits based on mutual understanding, intimacy and trust – occur more readily when relationships last. Hence the stress in this book on regular communication and long-term relationship stability, particularly with reference to establishing roots, and managing close relationships, as between soul mates.

DEALING WITH MEMORY

Memory is a powerful feature of relationships, and arises forcibly as an issue in handling bereavement, increasing security through reconciliation, and in cities, where yesterday's economic relationships survive in a literally concrete form.

Dealing with memory is crucial in forgiveness – between communities as well as individuals – because what's possible now in a given relationship will depend on how the two parties perceive and deal with past events. Also, relationships are not like marbles in a bag. They span time, overlap, and overflow into each other, so that even remote memories passed down as stories in families and communities can continue to exert a powerful influence over present relationships.

There is even a sense in which organisations have memories – or don't. On your second call to a technical helpline, you will usually have to supply your case number, because you're now talking to a different operative. Without the case notes from your last call, the operative (and by extension the whole helpline desk) will have no memory of the previous conversation, and everything will have to be started afresh from scratch.

LEARNING RELATIONAL SKILLS

It's not maths or literacy, but it's surely essential if you want to succeed in personal or organisational life. Relational skills are a key issue in schooling, in management, and in the constructive use of communications technology. People get more out of relationships if they know how to manage conflict without resorting to abuse or violence or withdrawal. Children learn these skills primarily at home, round the dinner table, in the give and take of family interaction.

The impact of this on business effectiveness two decades hence is one reason why companies should take more interest in the quality of workers' lives at home. Like it or not, most people don't just 'pick up' specific skills like self-disclosure, listening, commitment, or self-representation – though employees often perform better when they go on relationship awareness courses.

But, in sheer practical terms, is it possible to 'live relationally' in the twenty-first century Western world?

Even as summarised above, the heart of this book is more a philosophy than a fix. There's no single thing you can do, on a par with, say, reducing calorie intake, to prioritise relationships in your life. Whichever way you go, arranging your life in such a way that relationships work for you, and not against you, involves everything you do. It's a perspective, a framework for action.

If you're connected, directly or indirectly, to the busy professional and corporate world, you're not going to have much time. You'll have a demanding job, friends, perhaps a family, all sorts of ties that simultaneously define your existence and put you on a kind of treadmill. Making changes is tough.

As a first step, you might like to try reviewing your own relational world. The Relationships Foundation's website – www.relationshipsfoundation.org – has a special section dedicated to tools that can help you assess the state of your relationships. The site also has many other useful resources, including a discussion forum linked to the ideas discussed in this book (www.relationshipsfoundation.org/R_Option_discussion.html).

Almost inevitably, relationships are going to fall more and more under the spotlight as an issue in social organisation. Companies are increasingly recognising internal and external relationships as the key to competitive advantage. Questions of how relationships should be regulated are also being discussed in the context of public service delivery in schools, hospitals, and policing.

In other words, alongside the approach taken in this book, of individual relationship management, there is another approach of which the focus is public and organisational policy. And this is a thought to weigh carefully.

Take the Green Movement as an analogy. Just two years before her death in 1964, the ecologist Rachel Carson published *Silent Spring.* It was a revolutionary book, because it was the first to bring to public attention the idea that industrial processes – like the use of pesticides – could cause lasting damage to the environment.[1]

Forty years later, green thinking has imprinted itself on our consciousness. There is now a powerful political lobby representing environmental interests – meaning, broadly, the protection of the globe as a shared asset. And a sea-change has taken place in the values that govern our behaviour. Individually, we recycle. Collectively, we haggle over global warming, biodiversity and deforestation.

Environmentalism is impeccably PC. It is a matter of direct self-interest. And it retains a kind of ethical purity, even if, in practice, it produces some tricky ethical dilemmas.[2] Saving the planet is a good we can all safely agree on.

But environmentalism has one odd feature. Though you will instinctively support the green agenda, and may go to some trouble to put your old bottles in the right bin, you probably won't have suffered any direct consequences of environmental change. The odds are against your having contracted cancer as a result of the hole in the ozone layer. Most people have yet to wade through an ocean oil-spill. And until recently, even global warming hasn't represented much more than a rising line on a graph.

By contrast, changes in what we might call the *social ecology* – in the quality of our relationships – have impacted on us constantly, and often severely. We moan, privately between ourselves and publicly in the media, about the whole range of relational issues we've covered in the preceding chapters. We worry about rising levels of violent crime, the spread of communicable diseases, misunderstandings in communication, endlessly growing pressure on our time and the uncertain future for our children. Relationships are the substance of our connection, and the medium of our social ills. And yet, as a society, we simply haven't got to grips with the problem of relational breakdown.

The sociologist Robert Putnam has used the concept of social capital to highlight problems at a national level in the USA. The evidence of growing disconnectedness in Western societies, especially the USA, is overwhelming. But there is no obvious strategy – for individuals or for societies – to rebuild social capital.

That's why we say, quite candidly, that we think relationships are the coming political issue. They provide a language in which we can address, debate, and tackle the breakdown of social capital and the social problems that lie between us and the 'good society'.

They also underlie the entire environmental debate. Brazilian rainforests get bulldozed because of the economic relationships linking logging companies to international consumers. Whales flourish or are slaughtered, depending on whether we see our relationship with future generations as more, or less, important than the immediate relationships connecting commercial whalers to their markets. Relationships motivate conservation and exploitation.

In spite of all this, however, there are three reasons why it's still not quite respectable to argue for good relationships as a goal in the way we organise ourselves.

First, in a liberal society you'll have a real struggle with any idea that appears to threaten immediate and individual freedom of choice. Hence the problem with favouring marriage as a context for child-raising. As Melanie Phillips observed of a leading politician: 'He couldn't bring himself to say that if marriage was better for children, then other relationships were worse.'[3] The point here is not that marriage is *necessarily* the better alternative, but that ideology keeps us from squaring up to facts.

Second, there's a tendency to think that relationships have been accounted for already under the heading of social policy. Social democracy looks after our 'social' needs to the degree that this is affordable. The implication is that social issues are really about cash, and that going on about them marks you out as a blinkered old radical who won't see that you have to manage an economy, not mercilessly milk it. It's true, of course, that there is an argument to be had about how much national income should be creamed off to pay for social security. But relationship breakdown isn't income-specific. If affects everyone – rich and poor – and distributing public money for social ends only plugs one hole in the bucket. The difficulty, anyway, with social security expenditure is that so often it's applied as a sticking plaster to patch up the damage done by market forces – and does nothing to prevent further damage occurring. It's a system set up to chase its own tail. The relational approach, by contrast, seeks to build relationship priorities into the process of economic growth.

Third, some will point out that relationships have been breaking down since the year dot. We have always muddled through, and anyway, the overall direction of society isn't something we can do much about. Clearly, though, we don't take this rather limp attitude towards medical technology. We demand good physical health, and that demand translates into political commitment and public funding. Why are we so supine when it comes to improving what is the key indicator of our personal happiness – the quality of our relationships?

This, as they say, is the subject of another book – one which, as it happens, has already been written.[4] It is also the main concern of the Relationships Foundation, a Cambridge-based 'think and do tank' set up to examine the interplay of relationships and public policy. If you're interested in this wider picture, you'll find plenty of material on the Relationships Foundation website mentioned above (www.relationshipsfoundation.org), which demonstrates how to apply a relationships perspective to issues of public policy such as criminal justice, financial markets, and healthcare provision.

We are all making the future, whether we are aware of it or not. We make it by the values we choose, the behaviours we demonstrate, the political options we press for. Collectively we influence the course of history. You may not feel that your lifestyle decisions matter much in the broad run of things. But they do matter – for you, for the organisation where you work, and for the society we'll leave to the next generation.

---

1   Rachel Carson, *Silent Spring* (Boston: Houghton Mifflin Company, 1962).
2   Which, for example, is more important – jobs in the fishing industry, or preservation of stocks of North Sea cod?
3   Melanie Phillips, 'The relationship that dare not speak its name,' *Sunday Times,* 7 February 1999.
4   Michael Schluter and David Lee, *The R Factor* (London: Hodder & Stoughton, 1993). See particularly p.68ff. Copies of *The R Factor* can be ordered directly from the Relationships Foundation or through its secure website
      (www.relationshipsfoundation.org/books/Index.html). See overleaf for details.

VISIT OUR WEBSITE

www.relationshipsfoundation.org

[secure hosting]

To:

☑ Post your comments, personal stories and ideas about The R Option, and see what other readers say about it

☑ Join the Relationships Foundation's free mailing list and receive its regular briefings

☑ Find out more about the Foundation's work

☑ Access its resources on assessing relationships

☑ Order its books

☑ Make a financial contribution if you would like to support its work

"...Its main idea is here to stay."
(The Economist)

"There are a dozen or more tantalising proposals which deserve a wider airing..." (Financial Times)

"...many of the practical suggestions made are entirely sensible..."
(Times Literary Supplement)

The R Factor is the first book co-authored by Michael Schluter and David John Lee. Published in 1993, it offers a powerful critique of our culture and makes a compelling case for reconstructing much of our system around an understanding of the importance of relationships.

Essential reading for anyone interested in 'the big picture' and in social reform.

Only available from the Relationships Foundation.

To order your copy of **The R Factor**, contact the Relationships Foundation (see overleaf for details) or go to

www.relationshipsfoundation.org/books/The_R_Factor/Overview.htlm

SPECIAL OFFER:
Normally £7.99 (plus P&P) but anyone ordering through the website and quoting Order Code **ROR1** can buy it for only £5.99.

THE RELATIONSHIPS FOUNDATION

Jubilee House
3 Hooper Street
Cambridge CB1 2NZ
England

Tel. +44 (0)1223 566333
Fax. +44 (0)1223 566359

E-mail r.f@clara.net

www.relationshipsfoundation.org